Microsoft® Word 2010:

Level 2 of 3

JUDY MARDAR
PC Source

PAMELA R. TOLIVER
Soft-Spec

LABYRINTH
LEARNING™

El Sobrante, CA

Microsoft Word 2010: Level 2
by Judy Mardar and Pamela R. Toliver

Copyright © 2011 by Labyrinth Learning

LABYRINTH
LEARNING™

Labyrinth Learning
P.O. Box 20818
El Sobrante, California 24820
800.522.9746
On the web at lablearning.com

President:
Brian Favro

Product Development Manager:
Jason Favro

Managing Editor:
Laura A. Lionello

Production Manager:
Rad Proctor

eLearning Production Manager:
Arl S. Nadel

Editorial/Production Team:
Donna Bacidore, John Barlow,
Scott Benjamin, Belinda Breyer, Alec Fehl,
Sandy Jones, PMG Media

Indexing: Joanne Sprott

Interior Design:
Mark Ong, Side-by-Side Studios

Cover Design:
Words At Work

ITEM: 1-59136-308-X
ISBN-13: 978-1-59136-308-8

Manufactured in the United States of America.

10 9 8 7 6 5 4 3 2

Table of Contents

Quick Reference Tables

BUILDING BLOCK TASKS

GENERAL TASKS

GRAPHICS TASKS

LONG DOCUMENT TASKS

PAGE SETUP TASKS

Preface

Microsoft® Word 2010: Level 2 provides thorough training of Word 2010 intermediate skills. This course is supported with comprehensive instructor resources and our eLab assessment and learning management tool. And, our new work-readiness exercises ensure students have the critical thinking skills necessary to succeed to today's world. After completing this course, students will be able to successfully face the challenges presented in the next book in this series, *Microsoft Word 2010: Level 3*.

Visual Conventions

This book uses many visual and typographic cues to guide students through the lessons. This page provides examples and describes the function of each cue.

Type this text	Anything you should type at the keyboard is printed in this typeface.
	Tips, Notes, and Warnings are used throughout the text to draw attention to certain topics.
Command→ Command→ Command, etc.	This convention indicates how to give a command from the Ribbon. The commands are written: Ribbon Tab→Command Group→Command→ Subcommand.
FROM THE KEYBOARD Ctrl + S to save	These margin notes indicate shortcut keys for executing a task described in the text.

Exercise Progression

The exercises in this book build in complexity as students work through a lesson toward mastery of the skills taught.

- **Develop Your Skills** exercises are introduced immediately after concept discussions. They provide detailed, step-by-step tutorials.
- **Reinforce Your Skills** exercises provide additional hands-on practice with moderate assistance.
- **Apply Your Skills** exercises test students' skills by describing the correct results without providing specific instructions on how to achieve them.
- **Critical Thinking and Work-Readiness Skills** exercises are the most challenging. They provide generic instructions, allowing students to use their skills and creativity to achieve the results they envision.

A Note About Lesson and Page Numbering

You will notice that this book does not begin with Lesson 1 on page 1. This is not an error! The lessons in this book are part of a larger text. We have repackaged the large book into smaller books – while retaining the original lesson and page numbering – to accommodate classes of varying lengths and course hours.

All content in this book is presented in the proper, intended order.

6 Creating a Newsletter

LESSON OUTLINE

LEARNING OBJECTIVES

After studying this lesson, you will be able to:

- Insert section breaks in documents
- Use WordArt and clip art
- Create and manipulate newsletter-style columns
- Use building blocks
- Apply themes
- Insert pictures from files
- Edit pictures

In this lesson, you will use Word's Columns feature to create a newsletter. WordArt and clip art will add eye-appeal to the newsletter. You will also have an opportunity to work with Word's Building Blocks and Themes, which make creating professional-looking documents fast and easy. You will also work with basic picture-editing tools to add special touches to your graphics.

Creating a Client Newsletter

Welcome to Green Clean, a janitorial product supplier and cleaning service contractor to small businesses, shopping plazas, and office buildings. Green Clean uses environmentally friendly cleaning products and incorporates sustainability practices wherever possible, including efficient energy and water use, recycling and waste reduction, and reduced petroleum use in vehicles. In addition to providing green cleaning services, the company also sells its eco-friendly product directly to customers.

Jenna Mann is an administrative assistant for the Green Clean company. It is nearing the beginning of a new quarter, and Jenna is setting up the quarterly newsletter that will go to clients to keep them up to date on the happenings at Green Clean. Jenna will add pizzazz to the two-column newsletter by inserting WordArt and clip art images and using the Themes gallery to add color and other visual interest.

These are examples of WordArt and clip art.

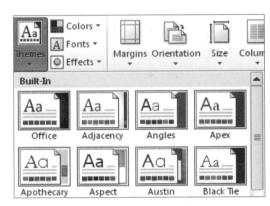

The Word Themes gallery provides a quick way to change a color scheme.

6.1 Working with Section Breaks

Video Lesson   labyrinthelab.com/videos

In Word, whenever you make a page-formatting change that doesn't apply to the whole document, you need one or more section breaks to define the portion of the document affected by the change. Changing margins is an example. If you have 1-inch margins in your document and you want a portion of the document to have 1.5-inch margins, you need one or more section breaks to separate that portion of the document. Otherwise, when you change the margins, they change for the entire document.

Inserting Section Breaks

You use Page Layout→Page Setup→Breaks ▤ to insert section breaks. There are four types of section breaks.

QUICK REFERENCE	WORKING WITH SECTION BREAKS
Type of Section Break	**Purpose**
Next Page	Inserts a section break and starts the new section on the next page
Continuous	Inserts a section break and starts the new section on the same page
Odd Page	Inserts a section break and starts the new section on the next odd numbered page; Word may feed a blank page to force the odd page section break
Even Page	Inserts a section break and starts the new section on the next even numbered page; Word may feed a blank page to force the even page section break

The example in this lesson is a columnar newsletter. The titles at the top of the document will be typed between the margins, which Word considers as just one column. Then the actual newsletter will be in two columns. This results in two separate sections. You display section numbers on the status bar by choosing Section from the pop-up menu when you right-click on the status bar.

The illustration on the next page shows the use of continuous section breaks that are sectioning off the two-column portion of a document.

Deleting Section Breaks

When you have the formatting marks turned on, a break is easily identified. Deleting a section break is as simple as clicking on it and tapping the [Delete] key. When you delete a section break, the section above the break takes on the same formatting as the section below the break.

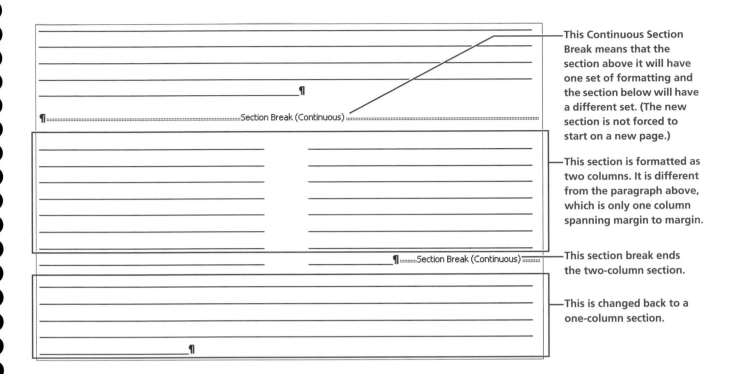

This Continuous Section Break means that the section above it will have one set of formatting and the section below will have a different set. (The new section is not forced to start on a new page.)

This section is formatted as two columns. It is different from the paragraph above, which is only one column spanning margin to margin.

This section break ends the two-column section.

This is changed back to a one-column section.

Insert a Section Break

In this exercise, you will begin developing a newsletter by inserting three title lines and a section break.

1. If necessary, start a **new** blank document, and then make sure the Word window is **maximized**.

2. If necessary, choose **Home→Paragraph→Show/Hide** ¶ from the Ribbon to display formatting marks.
   You need to display formatting marks in order to see a section break.

3. Type **Quarterly Newsletter** and **tap** Enter .

4. **Type** the following heading lines:

5. **Tap** Enter three times, then **right-click** the status bar and choose **Section** from the pop-up menu to display the section numbers on the status bar.

Insert a Continuous Section Break

6. Choose **Page Layout→Page Setup→Breaks** ▤ from the Ribbon, and then choose **Continuous** from the menu.

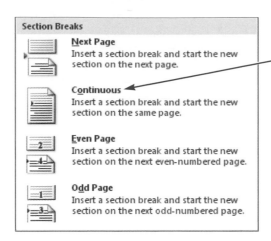

Now you can use different page formatting above and below the break.

Delete a Section Break

7. Position the **insertion point** on the Section Break and **tap** Delete.

8. Click **Undo** ↶ from the Quick Access toolbar to place the Section Break back into the document.

9. **Save** ▤ the file as **Green Clean Newsletter** in the Lesson 06 folder, and leave it **open** for the next exercise.

6.2 Using WordArt

Video Lesson   labyrinthelab.com/videos

Word provides a great tool, called WordArt, for creating smart-looking text objects. You can use the built-in designs as they are, or you can customize them.

Inserting WordArt

The Insert→Text→WordArt ◢ command reveals the WordArt gallery. Once you choose a style from the gallery, you can format and resize it. The following illustration displays the WordArt gallery.

Wrapping Text Around Objects

You edit and format WordArt objects using the WordArt Tools located on the Format contextual tab. Included in the formatting options is Text Wrapping, which controls the relationship of the text surrounding an object, such as a

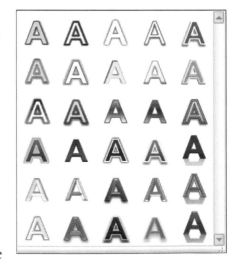

The WordArt gallery contains numerous styles with various preset colors.

WordArt object. Among the wrapping options are having the object move along with the text around it, using the In Line with Text option, or having the text stay in place by selecting the In Front of Text option, where you drag the object anywhere on the page.

The terms *object* and *image* are both used when referring to graphical elements such as WordArt, clip art, and pictures.

Notice the Drawing Tools→Format contextual tab that appears when a WordArt object is selected. It contains a wide variety of tools you can use to format a WordArt object.

The WordArt object has a series of circles and squares (selection handles) surrounding it that indicates the object is selected for your next command. The handles are used to resize the object.

A WordArt object must be selected to make the Format contextual tab visible.

Sizing WordArt

The small circles that surround an object when it's selected (selection handles) are also known as sizing handles. There is also a rotating handle. It is the small green circle at the top of the object. You can drag the rotate handle left or right to rotate the object.

You will also notice this rotating handle on other objects that you insert, such as clip art and shapes.

When you position the mouse pointer on a sizing handle, the pointer changes to a double-headed white arrow, which you can drag to increase or decrease the size of the object. Sizing from a corner handle changes the length and width relative to their original proportions.

The mouse pointer as it appears on a WordArt sizing handle

Insert and Edit a WordArt Object

In this exercise, you will use the newsletter title as the WordArt object. You will then wrap text around the WordArt object, change the background color, and add a text effect.

1. Select *Quarterly Newsletter* in the first line of the document, but do **not** select the paragraph mark at the end of the line.

2. Choose **Insert→Text→WordArt** ⒜ from the Ribbon, and then choose **Fill - Olive Green, Accent 3, Powder Bevel**.
    Notice the text is wrapped around the object. In this case, you do not want the text wrapped around; you want it on its own line. You will fix this problem next.

3. Make sure the object is still selected.

4. Choose **Drawing Tools→Format→Arrange→Wrap Text** ⒝ from the Ribbon.

5. Choose **In Line with Text** from the drop-down list.

Format the WordArt Object

First, you will change the WordArt fill color.

6. If necessary, select the **WordArt** object.

7. Follow these steps to change the WordArt object background color:

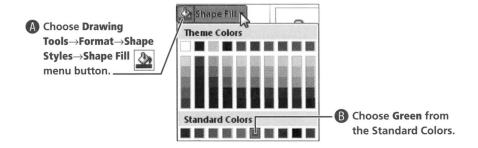

Ⓐ Choose **Drawing Tools→Format→Shape Styles→Shape Fill** menu button.

Ⓑ Choose **Green** from the Standard Colors.

8. Choose **Format→WordArt Styles→** 🅰 Text Fill ▾ menu from the Ribbon.

9. Choose **White, Background 1** from the Theme Colors group.
    Now you will add a text effect to the WordArt.

10. Choose **Format→WordArt Styles→Text Effects** 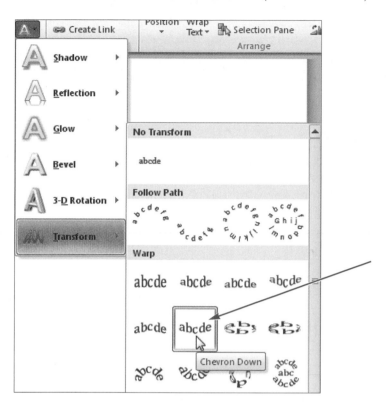 from the Ribbon, and then choose the **second effect** in the **second row** (Chevron Down) of the Transform group.

Format the Headings

Finally, you will center the headings and format the Green Clean heading.

11. Position the **insertion point** in the left margin area next to the WordArt object, then **click and drag down** to select it plus the other two headings.

12. Choose **Home→Paragraph→Center** 📧 from the Ribbon.

13. Format *Green Clean* with the **Cambria, Bold, 18 pt** font.

14. Compare your document headings with the illustration at the end of the exercise.

15. **Save** 💾 your document and leave it **open** for the next exercise.

6.3 Using Clip Art

Video Lesson   labyrinthelab.com/videos

Word 2010 includes a clip art collection installed on your hard drive. Even more clip art items are available online. Once you insert an image, you can change its size, degree of rotation, or location on the page.

Finding Clip Art

You insert clip art by choosing Insert→Illustrations→Clip Art 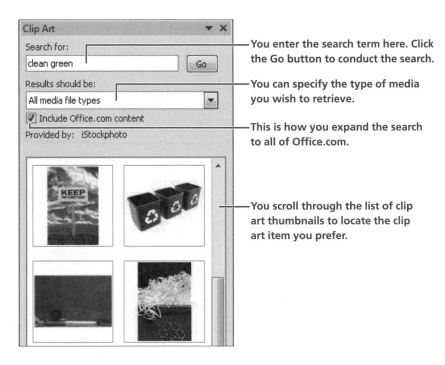 from the Ribbon. When you do so, Word displays the Clip Art task pane, where you can search for images by entering keywords. When you search for a keyword, the task pane displays thumbnails of all images located by your search. You can expand the search to include images on Office.com.

You enter the search term here. Click the Go button to conduct the search.

You can specify the type of media you wish to retrieve.

This is how you expand the search to all of Office.com.

You scroll through the list of clip art thumbnails to locate the clip art item you prefer.

Media Types

There are four media types to choose from:

- Illustrations—images drawn by graphic artists
- Photographs—photographic images
- Videos—simple animated pictures or brief video clips
- Audio—sound effects, such as the noise made by a car horn

Organizing Clip Art

The Clip Organizer is a special place to save your favorite images. It is found in the Microsoft Office Tools folder in Microsoft Office on the Start menu. You can copy and then paste the images directly into the Favorites collection in the Clip Organizer or use the File command in the Clip Organizer to pick and choose images you have saved on your computer. You can also create your own collection in the organizer to keep yourself more organized as you save more and more images.

QUICK REFERENCE	USING THE CLIP ORGANIZER
Task	**Procedure**
Open the Clip Organizer	■ Click the Start button. ■ Choose All Programs→Microsoft Office→Microsoft Office 2010 Tools from the menu. ■ Choose Microsoft Clip Organizer.
Copy a file into the Clip Organizer	■ Open the Clip Organizer. ■ Select the image in the document you will to place in the organizer. ■ Tap Ctrl+C. ■ Switch to the open Clip Organizer window. ■ Click the desired collection where to save the image. ■ Click Edit→Paste from the menu.
Add an image from within the Clip Organizer	■ Open the Clip Organizer. ■ Click on the collection (folder) in the left pane where you want to store the image. ■ Click File→Add Clips to Organizer from the menu. ■ Choose One of My Own. ■ Navigate to the file storage location. ■ Click the desired image to add to the organizer. ■ Click the Add button.

Sizing and Rotating Clip Art

Like WordArt, clip art has the sizing handles to rotate objects. As in WordArt, if you place the mouse pointer on a sizing handle, it changes to a double-headed white arrow, which you can drag to resize the object. You also can use the green circle rotate handle at the top of the selected image to rotate it.

The mouse pointer as it appears on a clip art sizing handle

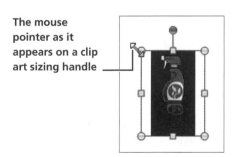

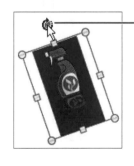

The mouse pointer as it appears on the clip art rotate handle

Moving Clip Art

When you insert clip art, it is positioned in line with text. This means you can use the left, right, or center alignment buttons in the Paragraph group on the Home tab of the Ribbon to reposition the image. However, if you want full control to move the clip art freely, you must change the layout mode to in front of text, found on the Wrap Text drop-down menu in the Arrange group on the Ribbon. To move the object by dragging, you point to the object until the mouse pointer becomes the four-headed arrow, and then drag it to a new location.

Four-headed arrow pointer shape to move a clip art or other object

QUICK REFERENCE	WORKING WITH CLIP ART
Task	**Procedure**
Insert clip art	Choose Insert→Illustrations→Clip Art ⊞ from the Ribbon.
Size clip art	With the object selected, place the mouse pointer on a sizing handle. When the pointer changes to a double-headed arrow, drag to resize the object.
Rotate clip art	With the object selected, place the mouse pointer on the green rotate handle. When the pointer changes to a circular arrow, drag right or left to rotate the object.

DEVELOP YOUR SKILLS 6.3.1
Insert and Resize Clip Art

In this exercise, you will search for a piece of clip art online and place it in your document. You will then resize the clip art image by using the Layout dialog box and by dragging a sizing handle. Finally, you will practice moving an object.

1. Click the **insertion point** next to the paragraph symbol below the Current Quarter heading.
   This is where you'll place your clip art image.

2. Choose **Insert→Illustrations→Clip Art** ⊞ from the Ribbon to display the Clip Art task pane.

3. Follow these steps to search for a piece of Clip Art:

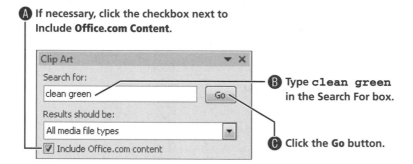

Ⓐ If necessary, click the checkbox next to Include **Office.com Content**.

Ⓑ Type `clean green` in the Search For box.

Ⓒ Click the **Go** button.

4. When the list of search results appears, **scroll** to locate the following clip art image. If this particular image is not available, choose a different image, preferably one that's appropriate for a newsletter from a "green" company.

5. Click directly on the **thumbnail image** to insert it in the document.
   The image could be very large or very small when you first insert it. This is due to how the original artwork was created. Most of the time, you will need to resize a clip art image once you have inserted it, just as you do here. You will resize it in the next section of this exercise.

6. Click the **Close** ☒ button in the upper-right corner of the Clip Art task pane.

7. If necessary, click the **View Ruler** ▣ button at the top of the vertical scroll bar to turn on the ruler.

Use the Layout Dialog Box to Resize an Image

8. Be sure the **image** is selected.

9. Choose **Picture Tools→Format→Size→dialog box launcher** ▣ to open the Layout dialog box.

10. Follow these steps to resize the clip art image:

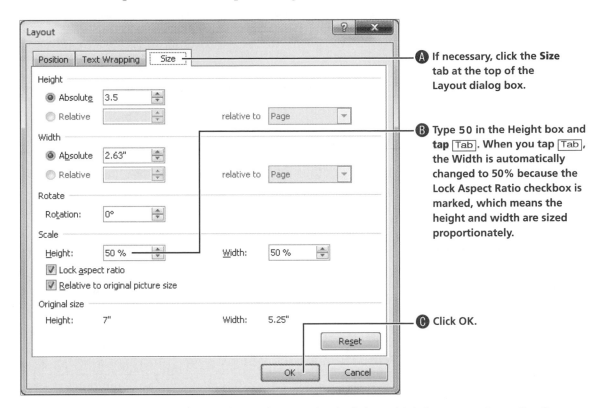

A **If necessary, click the Size tab at the top of the Layout dialog box.**

B **Type 50 in the Height box and tap ⌐Tab⌐. When you tap ⌐Tab⌐, the Width is automatically changed to 50% because the Lock Aspect Ratio checkbox is marked, which means the height and width are sized proportionately.**

C **Click OK.**

You can also use the spinner controls to change the height, which in turn automatically changes the width.

Resize an Image with a Sizing Handle

11. Follow these steps to resize the image to about 1 inch wide:

A **Position the mouse pointer on the sizing handle in the upper-left corner of the image. The pointer changes to a double-headed white arrow. (Note: Your double-headed arrow may appear black instead of white.)**

B **Press and hold the mouse button down, and drag diagonally toward the center of the image. You will see a shadow of the image as you drag it to its new size.**

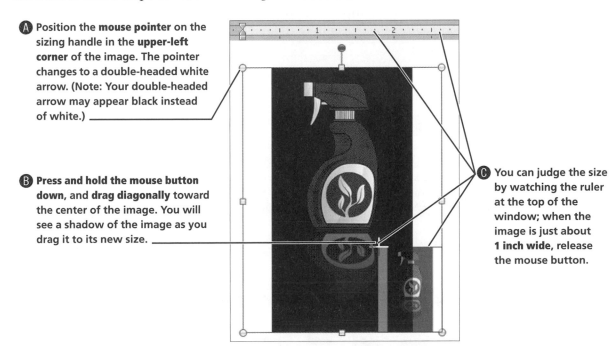

C **You can judge the size by watching the ruler at the top of the window; when the image is just about 1 inch wide, release the mouse button.**

When you resize using a corner sizing handle, the image retains its width-to-height ratio.

Move the Clip Art Image

12. Choose **Format→Arrange→Wrap Text** from the Ribbon.

13. Choose **In Front of Text** from the drop-down menu.

14. **Drag** the image to the center, and then **release** the mouse button.

15. **Undo** twice to move the image back to the left margin and change the text wrapping to In Line with Text.

16. Choose **Home→Paragraph→Center** to center the image on the page.

> ! NOTE
>
> If you used a clip art image other than the one shown above, size it so it's about two inches tall.

17. **Save** the file, and leave it **open** for the next exercise.

6.4 Working with Picture Styles

Video Lesson   labyrinthelab.com/videos

Using the Picture Styles is a quick way to enhance your images by adding borders, shadows, and directionality. There are many options from which to choose using the Picture Style gallery on the Format tab of the Picture Tools on the Ribbon. Picture Styles also include options to change border color, add special effects, and change the layout of an image. The Format tab is activated when a picture is selected.

Applying a Style

You can scroll through the selections in the gallery in the Picture Styles group, or click the More button to see the complete gallery. When you hover the mouse pointer over a style in the gallery, the image previews the new style; if you like it, simply click to apply the new Picture Style to the image.

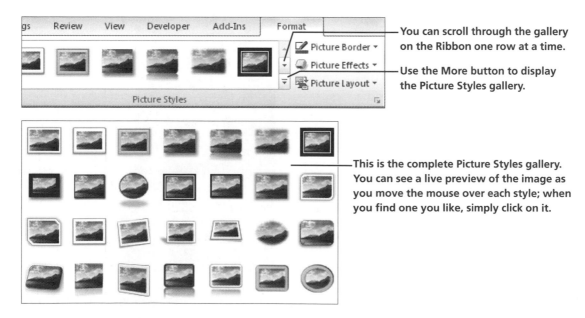

You can scroll through the gallery on the Ribbon one row at a time.

Use the More button to display the Picture Styles gallery.

This is the complete Picture Styles gallery. You can see a live preview of the image as you move the mouse over each style; when you find one you like, simply click on it.

Changing the Border Color on a Picture

The Picture Border colors are displayed by choosing Format→Picture Styles→Picture Border from the Ribbon. The Picture Tools tab is activated when an image is selected. You can choose a color from the Theme Colors group, which provides many shades of related colors, or from the Standard Colors group.

Choose from Theme Colors.

Choose from Standard Colors.

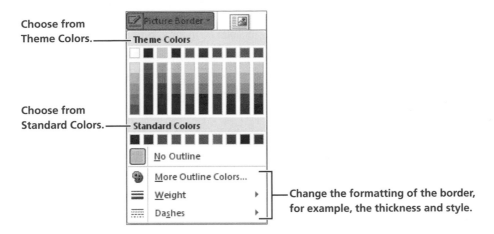

Change the formatting of the border, for example, the thickness and style.

Setting a Transparent Color

Pictures are made up of tiny pixels of many different colors. That is what causes shade variation in the graphic. When you click on a color in the object to make it transparent, all pixels of that same color are also made transparent. The mouse shape changes to a pen when you choose Set Transparent Color from the Colors drop-down menu in the Adjust group on the Ribbon.

Example of clip art image before making background transparent

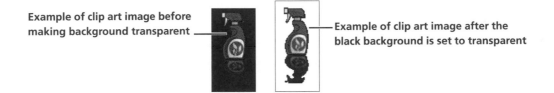

Example of clip art image after the black background is set to transparent

Applying an Artistic Effect

You can take your picture styling to the next level using special artistic effects. When an image is selected, a gallery of available artistic effects is found in the Adjust group on the Format tab under Picture Tools on the Ribbon. Some of the artistic effects include a pencil sketch, line drawing, a texturizer, and so forth.

QUICK REFERENCE	WORKING WITH PICTURE STYLES
Task	**Procedure**
Apply a style to clip art	■ Select the object, and then choose Format→Picture Styles from the Ribbon. ■ Click the desired style to apply it to the clip art.

QUICK REFERENCE	WORKING WITH PICTURE STYLES (continued)
Task	**Procedure**
Change the border color on a picture	■ Select the object, and then choose Format→Picture Styles→Picture Border from the Ribbon.
	■ Click the desired Theme or Standard color to apply it to the picture.
Set a transparent color	■ Select the object, choose Format→Adjust→Color from the Ribbon, and then choose Set Transparent Color from the drop-down menu.
	■ Click on the color on the image to make it transparent.
Apply an artistic effect	■ Select the object and choose Format→Adjust→Artistic Effects.
	■ Choose the desired effect from the gallery.

DEVELOP YOUR SKILLS 6.4.1
Format Pictures with Style

In this exercise, you will remove the black background from the image, add an oval frame around the clip art, and change the frame color to blue.

Set a Transparent Color

1. If necessary, select the **clip art image**.

2. Choose **Format→Adjust→Color** from the Ribbon.

3. Choose **Set Transparent Color** from the drop-down menu.
   Notice when you move the mouse pointer onto the document, it appears as a pen.

4. Click in the **black area** on the clip art image.
   The background around the image should now be white, and all you see is a green bottle and its shadow.

Add an Oval Frame Picture Style

5. If necessary, select the **clip art object**.

6. Follow these steps to apply a new style to the image:

Ⓐ Choose **Picture Tools→Format→Picture Styles** and then **scroll down** to the second row.

Ⓑ Click the **Beveled Oval, Black Picture Style** from the gallery.

Format the Border Color and Weight

7. Be sure the **object** is still selected.

8. Choose **Format→Picture Styles→Picture Border** from the Ribbon.

9. Follow these steps to change the border to a wide blue one:

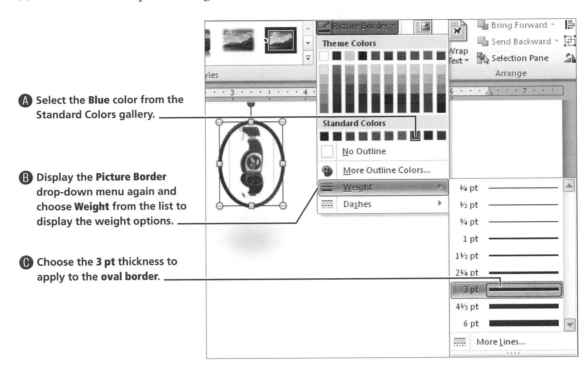

(A) Select the **Blue** color from the Standard Colors gallery.

(B) Display the **Picture Border** drop-down menu again and choose **Weight** from the list to display the weight options.

(C) Choose the **3 pt** thickness to apply to the **oval border**.

10. Save 💾 the file; leave it **open** for the next exercise.

6.5 Performing Basic Picture Editing

Video Lesson   labyrinthelab.com/videos

You can perform basic picture editing tasks with Word. For example, you can crop out parts of a picture. You can also rotate the image, adjust its brightness and contrast, and change its size without using a specialized image-editing program, such as Adobe Photoshop. If you aren't satisfied with the altered image, you can always reset the picture to its original form. If you want to perform more extensive editing to the image, you will need to use a special graphics program designed for that purpose, and then insert the finished image into Word.

Inserting a Picture from a File

In addition to being able to access photographs via the Clip Art task pane, you can also insert pictures directly from files. For example, you can insert a picture taken with a digital camera and stored on your computer or a graphic element copied from another source and saved on your computer.

Inserting a Screenshot

A screenshot is a picture of a complete or a portion of a screen. It can be a picture of the Windows Desktop, another Word file, or any other program window. For a shot of only a portion of the screen, you use Screen Clipping from the drop-down menu of the Screenshot command in the Illustrations group of the Insert tab. For a shot of a whole screen, you use the Screenshot command in the Illustrations group.

Insert a Picture from a File

In this exercise, you will insert a picture and display the Picture Tools Format tab.

1. If necessary, select the **clip art object** you placed in the document and **tap** Delete.

2. Choose **Insert→Illustrations→Picture**  from the Ribbon.

3. Navigate to the Lesson 06 folder, and **double-click** the GreenClean picture file to insert it.

4. Take a moment to practice with the picture's sizing handles and Rotate handle. After practicing, **rotate** and **resize** the image to its approximate original size and position. *Notice that when the picture is selected (handles visible), the contextual Format tab appears on the Ribbon. If you click away from the image, the contextual tab disappears.*

5. Click in the **document** to hide the contextual Format tab.

6. **Double-click** the image to display the Format tab in the foreground.

7. Leave the file **open** for the next topic.

Adjusting Brightness and Contrast

Video Lesson   labyrinthelab.com/videos

The brightness and contrast settings adjust how the picture appears on the screen and in print. You can use just one of these controls or both simultaneously. The Brightness and Contrast gallery is found on the Corrections drop-down menu in the Adjust group on the Ribbon. For more customized control, you can right-click the image and choose Format Picture to open the Format Picture dialog box.

- **Brightness**—This setting controls how bright each element in the picture looks. Turning up the brightness makes each element appear closer to white. Turning down the brightness makes each element appear closer to black.

- **Contrast**—This setting controls the difference between the darkest and lightest elements of the picture. A high-contrast image has elements that appear very white and very dark. A low-contrast image has elements that appear to have similar shades.

The original image

The same image with a -20% brightness and normal contrast setting

Cropping Pictures

Cropping allows you to hide parts of a picture. Choosing the Crop tool from Picture Tools→ Format→Size places crop handles around the object. You drag a handle to hide the unwanted portion of the picture. You can also uncrop a picture, if necessary. As you are cropping a picture, the part you drag over to crop out appears in a gray shadow until you click in the document; then the picture appears with only the part that you did not crop.

Cropping a picture in Word does not affect the original picture in any way. The area hidden by cropping is not deleted.

The image, displaying crop handles before cropping

The image after cropping with Crop handles visible

QUICK REFERENCE	WORKING WITH BASIC PICTURE EDITING TASKS
Task	**Procedure**
Insert a picture from a file	■ Position the insertion point where you want the picture to appear. ■ Choose Insert→Illustrations→Picture from the Ribbon. ■ Navigate to the desired picture, select it, and click the Insert button.
Insert a screenshot of a whole window	■ Have the program window you wish to capture open. ■ Choose Insert→Illustrations→Screenshot. ■ Choose the window to capture from the Available Windows menu.
Insert a partial screenshot of a window	■ Have the program window you wish to capture open. ■ Choose Insert→Illustrations→Screenshot menu button. ■ Choose Screen Clipping from the drop-down menu. ■ Choose the window to capture from the Available Windows menu. ■ Use the mouse to draw a rectangle around the portion of the window you wish to capture.

Task	Procedure
Adjust brightness and contrast	■ Select the picture to be adjusted. ■ If necessary, click the contextual Format tab to bring it to the foreground. ■ Click Corrections in the Adjust group, and then choose the desired effect from the gallery.
Crop or uncrop a picture	■ Select the picture to be cropped. ■ If necessary, click the contextual Format tab to bring it to the foreground. ■ Click the Crop ⬚ button in the Size group of the Format tab. ■ Place the mouse pointer on a handle on the picture, and drag to crop (or uncrop) the picture.
Undo picture adjustments	■ Select the picture that was modified. ■ If necessary, click the contextual Format tab to bring it to the foreground. ■ Click the Reset Picture ⬚ button in the Adjust group.

Compressing a Picture

Pictures and other graphics are usually very large, which increases the overall size of your Word document. Options for reducing the size of your document include compressing the selected image or all images in the document. Once images are compressed, it frees up room on your hard drive, or speeds up the download process on a web page. You can also choose whether to delete the portions of graphics that were cropped, which in turn frees up more space.

File Types to Compress

There are only certain types of graphics that can be compressed. Photographs and other high-resolution images are good examples of files that can be optimized, meaning the file size is reduced; they include .jpg, .tif, .bmp, and .png, to name a few. Others, such as drawing types with extensions such as .wmf, .emf, and eps, cannot be compressed.

You can use a graphics-editing program, such as Adobe Photoshop, to resize drawing images, and then use the Insert→Picture command to bring them into your Word document already optimized.

QUICK REFERENCE	COMPRESSING A PICTURE
Task	Procedure
Compress a picture	■ Double-click the picture to display the Format tab on the Ribbon. ■ Choose Format→Adjust→Compress Pictures to open the Compress Pictures dialog box. ■ Choose the desired compression options in the dialog box and click OK.

Edit a Picture

In this exercise, you will practice adjusting the brightness and contrast of a picture, and experiment with cropping and uncropping it.

1. Make sure the GreenClean picture is selected (handles are visible), and the contextual Format tab is in the foreground.

Preview Brightness Settings

2. Follow these steps to practice brightness adjustments:

Ⓐ Choose **Picture Tools→ Format→Adjust→Corrections button** to display the menu of options.

Ⓑ Hover the **mouse pointer** over the various settings, and Live Preview displays the brightness and contrast effects. Then **click** in the document to close the menu without making a change.

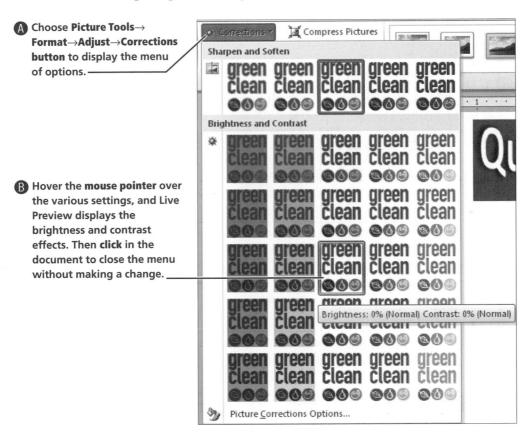

Crop the Image

3. Choose **Format→Size→Crop** from the Ribbon.

4. Follow these steps to crop the words *green clean* off the top of the image:

Ⓐ Notice the **cropping handles** that surround the image.

Ⓑ Move the **mouse pointer** to a corner handle, and notice that the pointer changes to a right angle.

Ⓒ Move the **mouse pointer** to the top-center cropping handle, and the pointer changes to a small upside-down T. **Click and drag down** until the words *green clean* are grayed out. Release the mouse button and click somewhere outside the picture.

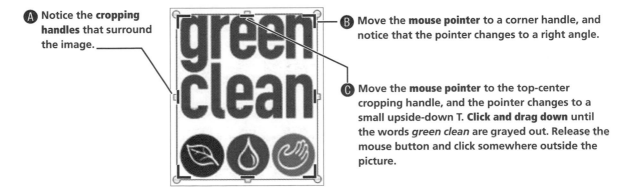

Uncrop the Image

When you crop an image in Word, the original is untouched. This makes it easy to uncrop the image later.

5. Select the **image** and choose **Picture Tools→Format→Size→Crop**, then **drag** the top-center handle again and **drag** it up to uncrop the image.

6. Click **Undo** 🔄 to crop the words out of the picture, and then click in the **document**. *Remember that cropped-out words are still part of the picture and, therefore, make the overall size of the file larger.*

Compress the Picture

Now you will delete the cropped-out portion of the picture to reduce the file size.

7. **Double-click** on the company logo to select it and display the **Picture Tools→Format** tab.

8. Choose **Format→Adjust→Compress Pictures** from the Ribbon.

9. Ensure there are **checkmarks** in the Apply Only to This Picture and Delete Cropped Areas of Pictures checkboxes; click **OK**.

10. **Save** 💾 the document and leave it **open** for the next exercise.

6.6 Working with Newsletter-Style Columns

Video Lesson   labyrinthelab.com/videos

You can use newsletter-style columns to arrange text in multiple columns. In a newsletter layout, text flows down one column and wraps to the top of the next column. Word automatically reformats column layout as you add or delete text.

Setting Up Columns

You choose Page Layout→Page Setup→Columns 🔲 to quickly specify the number or layout of your columns. When you specify the number of columns for the selected text, all columns are of equal width.

Customizing Column Widths

You can choose the More Columns command from the Columns menu to display the Columns dialog box, where you can set up more sophisticated column layouts. For example, you can insert a line between columns and customize the width of each column.

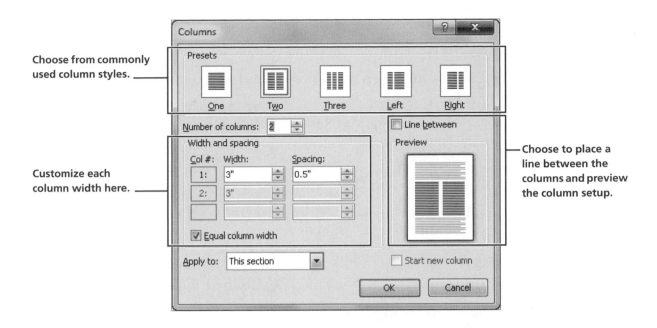

Choose from commonly used column styles.

Customize each column width here.

Choose to place a line between the columns and preview the column setup.

QUICK REFERENCE	WORKING WITH COLUMNS
Task	**Procedure**
Set up columns	■ Choose Page Layout→Page Setup→Columns from the Ribbon. ■ Choose the desired number of columns from the menu.
Insert a line between columns	■ Choose Page Layout→Page Setup→Columns from the Ribbon. ■ Choose More Columns from the menu. ■ In the Columns dialog box, check the Line Between checkbox.
Customize column widths	■ Choose Page Layout→Page Setup→Columns from the Ribbon. ■ Choose More Columns from the menu. ■ In the Columns dialog box, uncheck the Equal Column Width checkbox. ■ Use the spinner controls to change the size of column one; column two adjusts automatically then.

The appearance of the Columns button may vary based on your screen resolution.

DEVELOP YOUR SKILLS 6.6.1

Set Up Columns

In this exercise, you will open a document containing the content for your newsletter and copy it into the current document. Then you will format section two of your document with two columns, and finally you will insert a line between the columns.

1. **Open** the Newsletter Text file from the Lesson 06 folder.

2. **Tap** Ctrl + A to select the entire document.

3. **Press** Ctrl + C to copy the text of the document.

4. Switch back to the Green Clean Newsletter using the button on the **taskbar**.

5. Position the **insertion point** next to the paragraph mark under the section break.

6. **Tap** Ctrl + V to paste the newsletter text into your document.

7. Make sure the **insertion point** is in the second section of the document.

8. Choose **Page Layout→Page Setup→Columns** 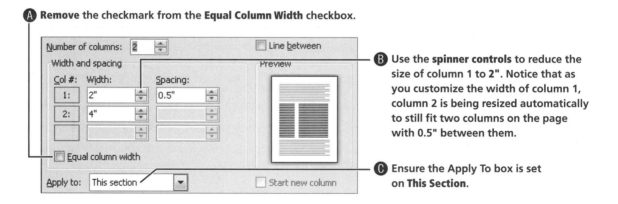 from the Ribbon, and then choose **Two** from the menu.
   The text of the newsletter is now arranged in two columns.

Add a Line Between Columns

9. Choose **Page Layout→Page Setup→Columns** from the Ribbon, and then choose **More Columns** from the menu to display the Columns dialog box.

10. Place a checkmark in the **Line Between** checkbox.

11. Click **OK** to insert the line and then click **Undo** to remove the line.

Customize Column Widths

12. Choose **Page Layout→Page Setup→Columns** from the Ribbon, and then choose **More Columns** from the menu to display the Columns dialog box.

13. Follow these steps to customize the column widths:

Ⓐ **Remove** the checkmark from the **Equal Column Width** checkbox.

Ⓑ Use the **spinner controls** to reduce the size of column 1 to 2". Notice that as you customize the width of column 1, column 2 is being resized automatically to still fit two columns on the page with 0.5" between them.

Ⓒ Ensure the Apply To box is set on **This Section**.

14. Click **OK**.
   The columns don't really look good this way, and while you could Undo 🔙 *at this point, if you changed your mind at a later time, there is still a very quick way to return the columns back to equal size.*

15. Choose **Page Layout→Page Setup→Columns** from the Ribbon, and then choose **More Columns** from the menu to display the Columns dialog box.

16. Click the checkbox next to **Equal Column Width**, and then click **OK**.

17. Scroll through the document to see how it looks.
   It looks like it would be a good idea to balance the columns on the second page. You will do that in the next topic.

18. **Close** the Newsletter Text file without saving, then **save** the Green Clean Newsletter file and leave it **open** for the next topic.

Working with Column Breaks

Video Lesson   labyrinthelab.com/videos

You can manually force a column to end by inserting a column break, thus moving text at the break point to the top of the next column. This technique is often used to place headings at the top of columns and to balance columns on the last page of a multicolumn document.

You insert column breaks by choosing Page Layout→Page Setup→Breaks ▤ from the Ribbon, and then choosing Column from the menu.

Column Breaks Compared to Section Breaks

You may recall that a section break designates the place in a document where some type of new page formatting begins. A column break gives you the ability to control the length of columns *within* a multicolumn section in a document.

QUICK REFERENCE	INSERTING COLUMN BREAKS
Task	**Procedure**
Insert a column break	■ Choose Page Layout→Page Setup→Breaks ▤ from the Ribbon. ■ Choose Column from the menu.

DEVELOP YOUR SKILLS 6.6.2
Insert and Remove a Column Break

In this exercise, you will balance your newsletter by inserting a manual column break.

1. Scroll to the bottom of **page 1**, and notice that the heading for the next paragraph is at the bottom of column 1.

2. Position the **insertion point** just in front of the *Wanting to Go Green, But Don't Know Where to Start?* heading.

3. Choose **Page Layout→Page Setup→Breaks** from the Ribbon, and then choose **Column** from the menu.
   This moves the Wanting to Go Green, But Don't Know Where to Start? *heading to the top of the next column.*

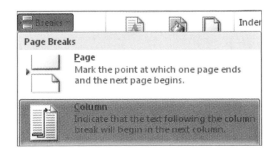

4. If necessary, choose **Home→Paragraph→Show/Hide** from the Ribbon to display the column break.

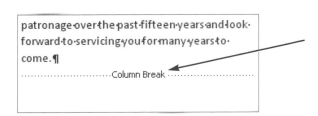

Delete the Column Break

5. Position the **insertion point** at the left end of the column break.

6. Tap ⌊Delete⌋ to remove the break.

7. Click **Undo** ↺ to reinstate the column break.

8. Save 💾 your newsletter, and leave it **open** for the next topic.

6.7 Using Building Blocks

Video Lesson labyrinthelab.com/videos

The Building Blocks feature allows you to insert pre-designed content into your documents, including cover pages, headers and footers, watermarks, equations, and blocks of text. You can choose from the many built-in Building Blocks, or you can transform your own frequently used content into custom Building Blocks. Building Blocks appear in various galleries throughout the Ribbon, such as cover pages and page numbers. You can modify existing Building Blocks, delete custom Building Blocks, and sort the list in various ways.

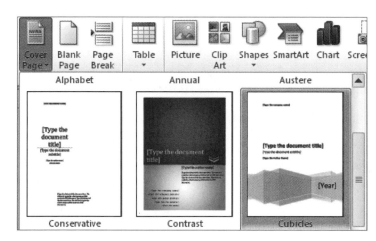

These predesigned cover pages in the Cover Page gallery are examples of Building Blocks.

Using Building Blocks Versus AutoCorrect

While both Building Blocks and AutoCorrect provide easy ways to insert often-used or large amounts of text or objects, the main difference between them is most noticeable in how you use them to insert something into a document. When you type an AutoCorrect name and tap ⌊Enter⌋, ⌊Tab⌋, or ⌊Spacebar⌋, or type a period or comma, the entry is automatically inserted into the document. However, typing a Building Block name requires you to perform another command to insert an entry. The following Quick Reference table explains the procedure for using either fabulous feature. Typically, though not always, Building Blocks are much larger entries, sometimes even a complete "boilerplate" document.

Task	Procedure
Insert an AutoCorrect entry	■ Type the AutoCorrect entry name. ■ Tap ⌈Spacebar⌉, ⌈Enter⌉, or ⌈Tab⌉, or type a period or a comma.
Insert a Building Block	■ Type the Building Block name. ■ Tap the ⌈F3⌉ key. *or* ■ Choose Insert→Text→Quick Parts 🗐 from the Ribbon, and then choose the entry from the list.
Insert a text box, header, footer, equation, or watermark Building Block using the Building Blocks Organizer	■ Choose Insert→Text→Quick Parts 🗐 from the Ribbon, and then choose Building Blocks Organizer from the menu, select the name in the list, and click Insert.
Insert a cover page Building Block	■ Choose Insert→Pages→Cover Page 🗐 from the Ribbon. ■ Choose the desired cover page from the gallery.

DEVELOP YOUR SKILLS 6.7.1

Use a Built-In Building Block

In this exercise, you will add a cover page Building Block to your newsletter.

1. Choose **Insert→Pages→Cover Page** 🗐 from the Ribbon.

2. When the cover page gallery appears, scroll down and choose the **Cubicles** cover page style shown here.

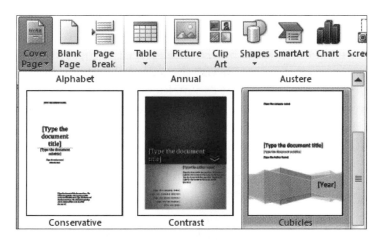

A cover page is attached to the beginning of the document.

Next you will type a title and subtitle, add a company logo for your cover page, and delete any unwanted objects from the cover page.

3. If necessary, click the **document title object**, as shown in the following illustration, and then type **Green Clean**.

4. Click the **document subtitle object** just below the title, and type **Environmentally Friendly Products and Practices**.

Delete Unwanted Objects

Now you will delete objects that you won't use on your cover page. There is an Author object just below the Subtitle object.

5. Click the object just **below** the subtitle object and you will see a tab labeled Author.

6. Click directly on the **Author** tab to select the object, as shown at right.

7. **Tap** the ⬚Delete⬚ key.

8. Choose **Home→Paragraph→Show/Hide** ¶ to turn off the formatting marks.

9. Use the same technique to delete the **Company** object in the upper-left corner of the page and the **Year** object in the bottom-right corner of the page.

10. **Save** 💾 the file, and leave it **open** for the next topic.

Creating Custom Building Blocks

Video Lesson labyrinthelab.com/videos

You can create your own custom Building Blocks. You select the content that you want to convert to a Building Block, and then you choose the Save Selection to Quick Part Gallery command on the Quick Parts menu. Content can include a wide variety of items such as text, a clip art image, or a WordArt object. You can also assign a custom Building Block to another gallery on the Ribbon. For example, if you created a cover page specific to your company, it would make sense to assign it to the Cover Page gallery.

Inserting a Building Block from the Quick Parts Gallery

The Quick Parts gallery in the Text group on the Insert tab of the Ribbon provides a convenient location for your custom Building Blocks. Inserting an item you saved in the Quick Parts gallery is as simple as clicking on it in the gallery.

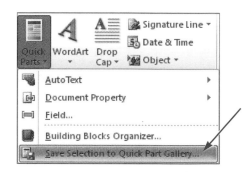

Modifying a Custom Building Block

There are two different types of modifications to Building Blocks: changing the properties or modifying the actual content and formatting. If you want to change the name, gallery, where to save it, and so forth, you do so in the Modify Building Block dialog box. However, if you want to modify the actual content, you make the desired changes, select the content, and save the selection with the same name. You will be asked if you want to redefine the existing entry.

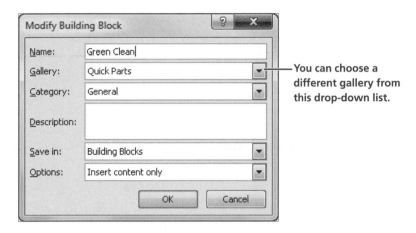

You can choose a different gallery from this drop-down list.

Create a Custom Building Block

In this exercise, you will type the contact information for the Green Clean company. You will then select it and save it to the Quick Parts gallery.

1. If necessary, choose **Home→Paragraph→Show/Hide** ¶ to turn on the formatting marks, and then **tap** Ctrl + End to place the insertion point at the end of the document.

2. Select the **first paragraph symbol** below the *Management Team and Strategy* paragraph. (If necessary, tap Enter to generate a paragraph symbol.)

3. Choose **Home→Paragraph→Line Spacing** from the Ribbon, and then choose **1.0** spacing.
   The menu closes.

4. Open the menu again, and choose **Remove Space After Paragraph**.

5. Choose **Home→Paragraph→Show/Hide** ¶ from the Ribbon to turn off formatting marks.

6. **Type** the following information:
   ```
   Green Clean
   719 Coronado Drive
   San Diego, CA 92102
   ```

7. Select the **three lines** that you just typed.

8. Choose **Insert→Text→Quick Parts** 🖼 from the Ribbon, and then choose **Save Selection to Quick Part Gallery**, as shown here.

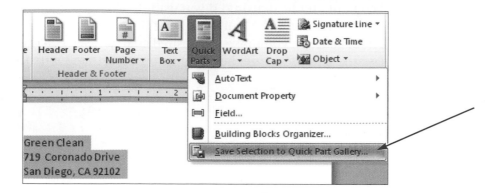

9. When the Create New Building Block dialog box appears, click **OK** to save the address information.

Insert the Custom Building Block

Now you will delete the address from the newsletter so you can test your new Building Block.

10. Make sure the address is still selected, and then **tap** Delete to remove it.

11. Choose **Insert→Text→Quick Parts** 🖼 from the Ribbon, and then click your new **Building Block** at the top of the menu to insert it in the document.

Modify Building Block Properties

12. Choose **Insert→Text→Quick Parts** 🖼 from the Ribbon.

13. **Right-click** the Green Clean Building Block at the top of the list, and choose **Edit Properties** in the menu to open the Modify Building Block dialog box.

14. Follow these steps to change the name of the Building Block:

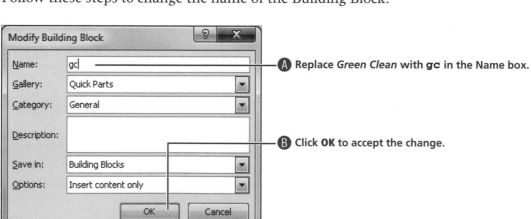

15. Click **Yes** in the message box asking if you want to redefine the entry.

Modify Building Block Contents

16. Position the **insertion point** at the end of the street address, **tap** the Spacebar, and type **Suite 200**.

17. **Double-click** on the zip code in the address in the document at the bottom of the page and type **92108**.

18. Select the **three-line** name and address.

19. Choose **Insert→Text→Quick Parts** from the Ribbon, and then choose **Save Selection to Quick Parts Gallery**.

20. Type **gc** for the Building Block name and click **OK**.

21. Click **Yes** in the message box to redefine the entry.

22. If necessary, select the **three-line** name and address at the bottom of the column and **tap** Delete.

23. **Save** your newsletter, and leave it **open** for the next exercise.

Sorting the Building Blocks List

Video Lesson | labyrinthelab.com/videos

When you open the Building Blocks Organizer, you can sort the list using any of the column headings. Click a heading to sort in Ascending order.

Deleting a Custom Building Block

You delete a Building Block through the Building Blocks Organizer. You can also insert a Building Block from within the Organizer and edit building block properties.

You can click any of the column headings to sort the list.

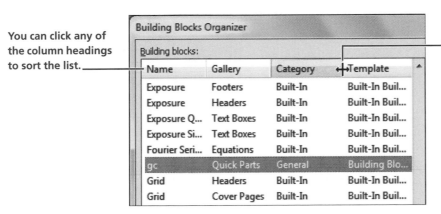

To modify a column width, place the mouse pointer on the border between two columns; the mouse pointer changes to a double-headed arrow. You can then press and hold the mouse button and drag to the left or right to narrow or widen the column.

DEVELOP YOUR SKILLS 6.7.3

Delete a Custom Building Block

In this exercise, you will practice sorting the Building Blocks list and then delete the Building Block you created in the preceding exercise.

1. Choose **Insert→Text→Quick Parts** ▦ from the Ribbon.

2. Follow these steps to begin the deletion:

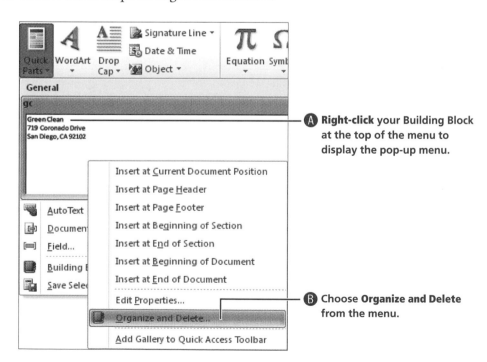

Ⓐ **Right-click** your Building Block at the top of the menu to display the pop-up menu.

Ⓑ Choose **Organize and Delete** from the menu.

The Building Blocks Organizer appears with the Green Clean Building Block highlighted in the list.

3. Click the **column headers** for each column, ending with Name column.

4. Scroll, if necessary, to locate and select the **gc** Building Block.

5. Click the **Delete** button at the bottom of the dialog box to delete the item.

6. When the message box appears verifying that you want to delete the Building Block, click **Yes**.

7. Click the **Close** button in the bottom-right corner of the dialog box.

8. **Save** 🖫 your newsletter, and leave it **open** for the next exercise.

Working with Preformatted Text Boxes

Video Lesson   labyrinthelab.com/videos

A preformatted text box is a box that you can type text in. However, the big difference is that it is already preformatted for you. Perhaps you have seen a quote in a magazine set in the middle of a page or some extra information the author wants to stand out from the rest of the article. These are referred to as pull quotes and sidebars. When you insert a preformatted text box, it has a designated place on the page and will be inserted on the page where the insertion point is located, if there is room; otherwise, it will be placed on a new page. You may move and resize the text box once it is inserted. When you type in it, the text will be wrapped automatically. The preformatted text boxes are found in the Building Blocks Organizer.

QUICK REFERENCE	INSERTING A PREFORMATTED TEXT BOX
Task	**Procedure**
Insert a preformatted text box	■ Choose Insert→Text→Quick Parts 🔲 from the Ribbon. ■ Choose Building Blocks Organizer from the menu. ■ Select the desired text box, and then click Insert. ■ Move or resize the text box as desired after it is inserted in the document. ■ Type the desired text in the box.

DEVELOP YOUR SKILLS 6.7.4
Insert a Preformatted Text Box

In this exercise, you will insert a pull quote preformatted text box. You will then resize and move it, and finally type a testimonial from a customer in it.

1. Tap [Ctrl]+[End] to ensure the insertion point is at the bottom of the document.

2. Choose **Insert→Text→Quick Parts** 🔲 from the Ribbon.

3. Choose **Building Blocks Organizer** from the menu.

4. Follow these steps to insert the Mod Quote text box:

Ⓐ Click the **Name** column heading to sort the Building Blocks list in ascending order.

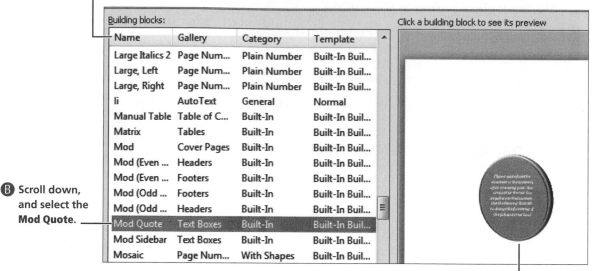

Ⓑ Scroll down, and select the **Mod Quote**.

Ⓒ View the style and location of the preformatted text box. Notice the text box is formatted in an oval and is located in the middle of the page.

5. Click the **Insert** button.
Don't worry about where the pull quote text box is located for the moment. You will enter text in the box, and then resize and move it to a better location.

6. Begin **typing** (you do not have to click it first) the following in the text box:

`We appreciate all you do for us AND for our environment!`
`Thank you for such excellent customer service.` `Enter`

`Daniels & Daniels, Inc.`

Format the Text in the Text Box

7. Select the text in the **pull quote**.

8. Using the Mini toolbar, change the Font Size to **10**.
Because it is smaller now, pull quote will fit on the previous page in the middle, where it was preformatted to go.

Resize the Text Box

9. Follow these steps to reduce the size of the text box:

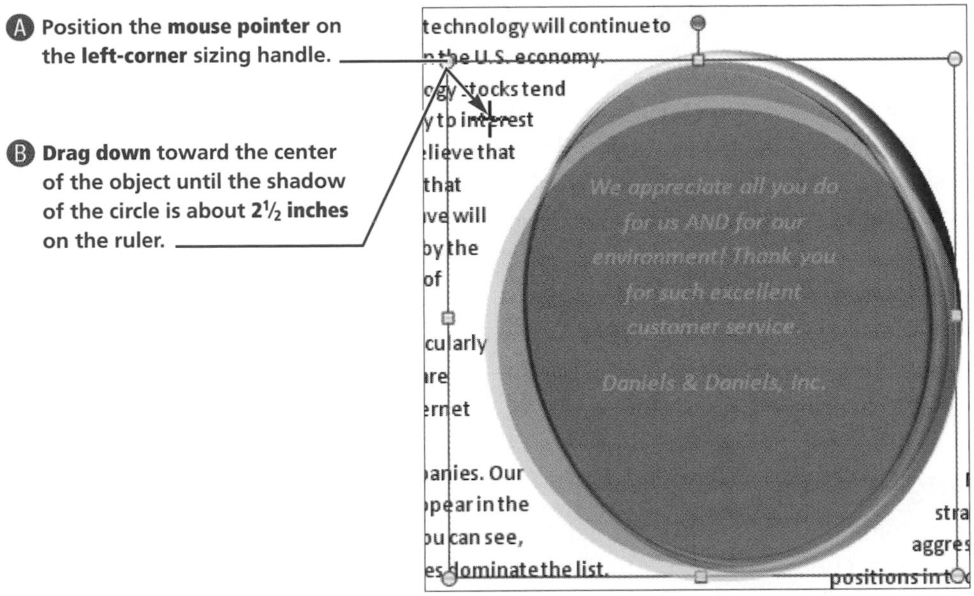

A Position the **mouse pointer** on the **left-corner** sizing handle.

B **Drag down** toward the center of the object until the shadow of the circle is about 2½ **inches** on the ruler.

[Text partially obscured by circle graphic:]
technology will continue to ... the U.S. economy. ...ogy stocks tend ...y to interest ...lieve that ...that ...ve will ...by the ...of ...cularly ...re ...rnet ...anies. Our ...pear in the ...u can see, ...es dominate the list.

We appreciate all you do for us AND for our environment! Thank you for such excellent customer service.

Daniels & Daniels, Inc.

stra
aggres
positions in t

Move the Text Box to a Different Location

Next, you will move the text box to a more appropriate location for this document. Also, don't be surprised if you need to tweak the size slightly; it's a little difficult to judge the size when you cannot see the text while you are resizing the object.

10. If necessary, **scroll up** to see that the preformatted text box has automatically moved up to the middle of the third page.

    The object moved here because it was preformatted to be located in the middle of the page. You will move it now to the empty space at the bottom of the right-side column on page 3.

11. Select the **text box**.

12. Position the **mouse pointer** on the edge of the text box so it becomes the four-headed arrow.

13. Drag the **text box** down to the bottom of the column as shown in the illustration, and then release the mouse button.

14. If necessary, **resize** the text box to display all the text inside it.

15. **Save** 💾 the document and leave it **open** for the next topic.

addition, we will maintain an appropriate level of diversification in bonds, cash, cash equivalents, and REIT's (Real Estate Investment Trusts).

We appreciate all you do for us AND for our environment! Thank you for such excellent customer service.

Daniels & Daniels, Inc.

6.8 Applying Themes

Video Lesson   labyrinthelab.com/videos

Word has a great feature that can instantly add color and visual variety to your documents. A *Theme* is a combination of colors, fonts, and graphic elements that you can apply to any document. You apply Themes from the Themes Gallery in the Themes group of the Page Layout tab. When you hover the mouse pointer over a Theme in the gallery, Live Preview displays the effect of the Theme before you apply it.

Customizing a Theme

You can customize any Theme to match your creative side. You can change the colors in a Theme, choose new fonts, and even add Theme effects such as line thickness, fill color, and so forth.

Changing Theme Colors

Built-in color schemes in a Theme have been coordinated to work together. You can modify the colors using Theme Colors in the Themes group on the Page Layout tab of the Ribbon. When you change a Theme color, it does not change the built-in Theme; it only modifies the colors in your current document. The colors not only affect the font color, but colors in tables, drawing shapes, and charts are all part of the schemes as well.

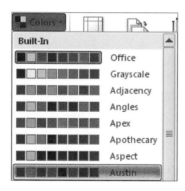

Each one of these sets is a complete color scheme affecting text and fill colors in your document.

Changing Theme Fonts

Themes are created using a set of coordinated fonts. A Theme font set includes either a specific font type in two different sizes for the heading and body text or two different fonts that blend nicely. The Theme Fonts gallery is found in the Themes group on the Page Layout tab of the Ribbon.

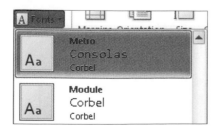

Font sets may include the same font of different sizes or two different fonts.

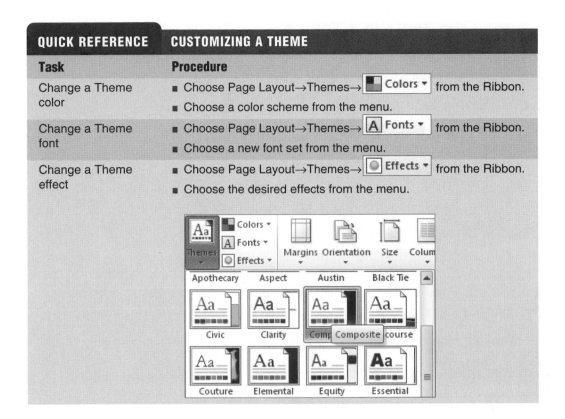
DEVELOP YOUR SKILLS 6.8.1

Apply a Theme to Your Newsletter

In this exercise, you will use Live Preview to examine a variety of Themes, and then you will apply a Theme to your newsletter.

1. **Scroll up** to the cover page and make sure the titles are visible on the screen.
   The effect of Themes will be particularly easy to see on this page.

2. Choose **Page Layout→Themes→Themes** from the Ribbon to display the Themes gallery.

3. Hover the **mouse pointer** over several different Themes and observe the changes in your document.

4. Click the **Composite Theme** (the third one in the third row) to apply it to the document.

5. **Scroll** through your document to see the impact of the new Theme.

Change the Theme Colors

6. Scroll to the **last page** to view the color change in the chart and table.

7. Choose **Page Layout→Themes→ Colors** from the Ribbon.

8. Move the **mouse pointer** around several of the color schemes to view the Live Preview in your document.

9. Choose **Civic** from the menu.

Change the Fonts in a Theme

10. Scroll to the **first page** to view the font changes in the title and subtitle.

11. Choose **Page Layout**→**Themes**→ A Fonts ▾ from the Ribbon.

12. **Scroll** through the list of font sets to view the Live Preview.

13. Choose the **Metro** font set for your document.

14. **Scroll** through the document to view the font and color changes in the document.

15. **Save** 💾 the file, and leave it **open** for the next topic.

Resetting a Theme

You can always return to the original look of your document by choosing Reset to Theme from Template from the bottom of the Themes menu, as shown in the following illustration. On the other hand, if you simply want to apply a different Theme, it isn't necessary to reset it first. You can just apply one Theme after another, thus overriding the previous Theme.

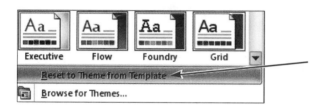

DEVELOP YOUR SKILLS 6.8.2

Reset the Theme

In this exercise, you will reset the document back to its original look.

1. Choose **Page Layout**→**Themes**→**Themes** 🅰 from the Ribbon to display the menu.

2. Choose **Reset to Theme from Template** at the bottom of the menu.

3. **Scroll** through the document and observe the original colors and fonts.

Inserting Drop Caps

Video Lesson   labyrinthelab.com/videos

A Drop Cap command creates a large first letter of a paragraph. You have the option of leaving it in the paragraph itself with the text wrapped around it, or placing the large letter out in the margin next to the paragraph. Other options include changing the font for the drop cap, modifying the number of lines to drop, and setting the distance from the other text. You must be careful to select only the first letter of a word before applying a drop cap to it. If you select the entire word, the Drop Cap command will make the entire word very large.

—This is an example of a drop cap within the paragraph with the rest of the text wrapped around it.

We have exciting news to share! After experiencing much success in the Richmond Metropolitan area, Green Clean has decided to expand into the Charlottesville area. The expansion will include new office space, ergonomically correct, of course, and a brand new retail facility to house all our earth-friendly products. We hope to be up and running in Charlottesville by mid-year. Naturally, we will continue our excellent customer service here in the Richmond market without any interruption in service.

—This is an example of a drop cap set out in the margin. Notice that the text does not wrap around the drop cap.

We have exciting news to share! After experiencing much success in the Richmond Metropolitan area, Green Clean has decided to expand into the Charlottesville area. The expansion will include new office space, ergonomically correct, of course, and a brand new retail facility to house all our earth-friendly products. We hope to be up and running in Charlottesville by mid-year. Naturally, we will continue our excellent customer service here in the Richmond market without any interruption in service.

DEVELOP YOUR SKILLS 6.8.3

Insert a Drop Cap

In this exercise, you will insert drop caps in the newsletter

1. Scroll to **page 2** and select the *W* in the word *What's* in the first column on the left.

2. Choose **Insert→Text** from the Ribbon.

3. Follow these steps to apply the Drop Cap feature:

Ⓐ Click the **Drop Cap** button in the Text group on the Ribbon.

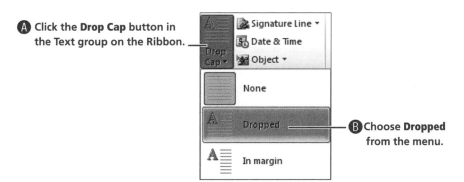

Ⓑ Choose **Dropped** from the menu.

4. **Save** 💾 the file, and leave it **open**.

6.9 Working with Views

Video Lesson   labyrinthelab.com/videos

Word lets you view your document in several ways. Each view is optimized for specific types of work, thus allowing you to work efficiently. The views change the way documents appear on the screen but have no impact on the appearance of printed documents. You can choose the desired view from the View tab on the Ribbon or from the View buttons at the right end of the status bar at the bottom of the Word window.

Document views that appear on the View tab of the Ribbon

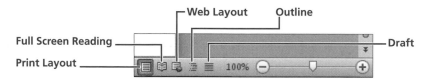

View buttons that appear at the bottom-right side of the Word window

DOCUMENT VIEWS	
View	**Description**
Print Layout	This is the default view in Word 2010. In this view, documents look very similar to the way they will look when printed. It is the most versatile view, allowing you to see such things as graphics, headers and footers, and multicolumn layout. You will probably use this view most of the time.
Full Screen Reading	Full Screen Reading makes it easy to read documents on the screen. It removes elements such as the Ribbon and the status bar in order to display more of your document. This view contains the View Options button, which offers varying display options within the window.
Web Layout	Web Layout displays your document as it would look as a web page. Text, graphics, and background patterns are visible. The document appears on one long page without page breaks.
Outline	Outline view is useful for organizing long documents.
Draft	This view simplifies page layout by eliminating elements such as headers and footers, graphic elements, and the display of multiple columns. This view can be useful when you want to focus on content and ignore surrounding elements.

Change the View

In this exercise, you will try out various views available in Word. You may wish to refer to the view descriptions in the previous table as you look at the view.

1. Locate the buttons ▣▤▥▤▤ at the right end of the **status bar** at the bottom of the window.
   The first button is the Print Layout button, which is the current view.

2. Click the second button, **Full Screen Reading** ▤, and your newsletter will look quite different.
   The column layout may not display accurately in this view. If not, you'll see how to change that in the next steps.

3. Click the **View Options** ▤ button in the upper-right corner of the screen.

4. Choose **Show Printed Page** from the menu if the feature is not turned on. (The icon will have a yellow highlight if it's turned on.)

5. Click the **Next Page** ▶ button at the top-middle section of the screen.
   Now your columns are visible.

6. Click the **View Options** ▤ button again, and click **Show Printed Page** again to turn off the view.

7. Click the **Close** ✖ button in the upper-right corner of the screen to return to Print Layout view.

8. Click the **View** tab and notice the corresponding views in the Document Views group.

9. Click **Full Screen Reading** ▤ in the Document Views group.

10. Click the **Close** ✖ button in the upper-right corner of the window to return to Word's default view.

Using Zoom Controls

Video Lesson   labyrinthelab.com/videos

The Zoom commands in the Zoom group of the View tab provide the ability to change the magnification of your document and control the number of pages that you can display at one time on the screen.

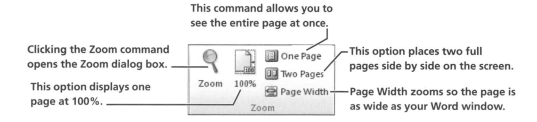

Clicking the Zoom command opens the Zoom dialog box.

This command allows you to see the entire page at once.

This option displays one page at 100%.

This option places two full pages side by side on the screen.

Page Width zooms so the page is as wide as your Word window.

In the Zoom dialog box, you can choose from preset degrees of magnification or specify your own. You can also control the number of pages to display at one time.

You click one of these option buttons to choose a preset degree of magnification.

You can use the spinner controls in the Percent box to choose a customized percent of magnification.

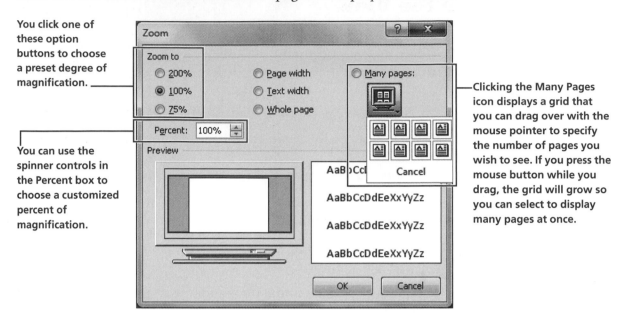

Clicking the Many Pages icon displays a grid that you can drag over with the mouse pointer to specify the number of pages you wish to see. If you press the mouse button while you drag, the grid will grow so you can select to display many pages at once.

The Zoom bar in the bottom-right corner of the Word window provides a quick way to change your document's magnification.

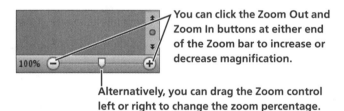

You can click the Zoom Out and Zoom In buttons at either end of the Zoom bar to increase or decrease magnification.

Alternatively, you can drag the Zoom control left or right to change the zoom percentage.

QUICK REFERENCE	SETTING DOCUMENT VIEWS
Task	**Procedure**
Change the document view	■ Use the View buttons on the right side of the status bar. *or* ■ Choose View→Document Views from the Ribbon, and click the desired view in the group.
Zoom the view	■ Use the Zoom bar on the right side of the status bar to change magnification. *or* ■ Choose View→Zoom from the Ribbon, and click the desired option from the group.

Use the Zoom Controls

In this exercise, you will use your newsletter to practice with the Zoom controls.

1. Position the **insertion point** at the top of the page following the cover page.

2. Choose **View→Zoom→Zoom** 🔍 from the Ribbon.

3. Follow these steps to display all three pages of the newsletter at once:

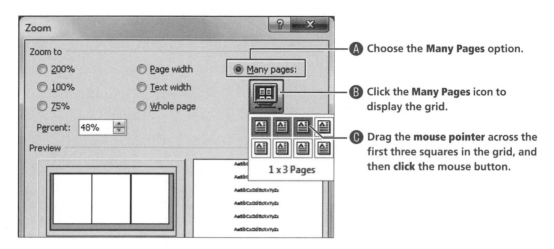

4. Click **OK** to view the three pages.

5. Take a moment to test the other options in the Zoom group on the Ribbon, and then choose the **One Page** button.
Next you'll test the zoom bar in the bottom-right corner of the Word window.

6. Follow these steps to change magnification via the zoom bar:

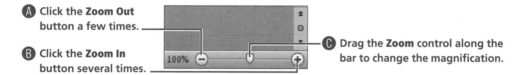

7. Return the magnification to **100%** using the controls on the Zoom bar.

8. **Save** 💾 your file, and **close** it.

6.10 Concepts Review

Concepts Review labyrinthelab.com/word10

To check your knowledge of the key concepts introduced in this lesson, complete the Concepts Review quiz by going to the URL listed above. If your classroom is using Labyrinth eLab, you may complete the Concepts Review quiz from within your eLab course.

Reinforce Your Skills

Produce a Winter Holiday Newsletter

In this exercise, you will create a newsletter with a WordArt heading, a section break, and a two-column layout. Then you will add a cover page and modify the Theme.

1. Start a **new** blank document.

2. If necessary, click the **Show/Hide** ¶ button to display formatting characters.

Insert WordArt

3. Choose **Insert→Text→WordArt** 🅰 from the Ribbon and choose the option in the **first column** in the **first row** (Fill - Tan, Text 2, Outline - Background 2).

4. Choose **Format→WordArt Styles→Text Effects** from the Ribbon.

5. Choose **Transform** from the menu, and then select **Warp→Chevron Up** from the gallery.

6. Select the **text** in the WordArt object, type **The Hope Report**, and click **outside** the object to view the new effect.

7. Select the **WordArt object**, and then choose **Format→Shape Styles→Shape Fill** 🎨 **menu ▾** from the Ribbon.

8. Click a color of your choice to change the WordArt color.

Insert a Continuous Section Break

9. **Double-click** in the document right under the WordArt object and **tap** Enter.

10. Choose **Page Layout→Page Setup→Breaks** ▤ from the Ribbon.

11. Choose **Continuous** from the menu.

12. Select the **WordArt object**, and drag it over to the center of the page and down just a little from the top of the page.

Insert the Newsletter Text

13. Position the **insertion point** next to the paragraph symbol below the section break.

14. **Open** the rs-New Year document from your Lesson 06 folder.

15. Use Ctrl + A and then Ctrl + C to select and copy the entire document.

16. Switch back to your new document using the button on the **taskbar**.

17. Use Ctrl + V to paste the text.

18. Make sure the **insertion point** is in the second section of the document.

19. Choose **Page Layout→Page Setup→Columns** ▦ from the Ribbon.

20. Choose **Two** from the menu.

Insert a Cover Page

21. Choose **Insert→Pages→Cover Page** ⬚ from the Ribbon.

22. **Scroll down** and click the **Mod** design to add a cover page to your newsletter.

23. **Scroll up** and click the **Title** object, then type **The Hope Report** in the Title box of the cover page.

24. Hover the **mouse pointer** over the line below the title, which reads *Type the Document Subtitle.*

25. Click the **object**, and then type **December 2012**.

Delete Unnecessary Objects

26. **Click** the object beginning with the text *Type the abstract....*

27. Click directly on the tab labeled **Abstract** to select the entire object, and then **tap** the ⌷Delete⌷ key.

28. Use the same technique to delete the next two objects, the **Author** and **Date** objects.

Apply a New Theme

29. Choose **Page Layout→Themes→Themes** ⬚ from the Ribbon.

30. Click the **Verve** theme in the gallery to apply it to your newsletter.
Notice the color and font changes that are applied to the newsletter.

Insert a Column Break

31. Position the **insertion point** to the left of the heading *What a Magic Show!*

32. Choose **Page Layout→Page Setup→Breaks** ⬚ from the Ribbon.

33. Choose **Column** from the menu to move the heading and its entire paragraph to the top of the second column.

Insert Drop Caps

34. Select the *T* in the word *This* in the first paragraph.

35. Choose **Insert→Text→Drop Cap** from the Ribbon.

36. Choose **Dropped** from the menu.

37. Using the same technique, insert a **dropped cap** for the *O* in the word *Our* in the first paragraph of the second column.

38. **Close** the rs-New Year document without saving any changes.

39. **Save** ⬚ the document as **rs-Hope Report**, and then **close** it.

Create a Real Estate Newsletter

In this exercise, you will convert a document to a newsletter format and insert a section break and clip art.

1. **Open** rs-RE News from your Lesson 06 folder.

2. If necessary, click the **Show/Hide** ¶ button to display formatting characters.

3. Position the **insertion point** to the left of the heading *How the Market Looks*.

4. Insert a **continuous** section break.

5. Select the **first heading line** at the top of the document, and format it with Cambria (Headings) bold 20 pt.

6. Format the **second line** with Cambria (Headings) italic 14 pt.

7. **Center** both heading lines.

Use and Format a Column Layout

8. Click the **insertion point** in the second section of the document, and apply a **two-column layout** to the text.

9. Format the four headings in the second section with **bold 12 pt**.

10. Position the **insertion point** to the left of the heading *Increase the Value of Your Home* in the first column.

11. Insert a **column** break to place the heading and its entire paragraph in column 2.

Insert and Format a Picture

12. Make sure the **insertion point** is at the top of the second column, and **tap** Enter to create a blank line.

13. Place the **insertion point** on the blank line, and then insert a **clip art picture** of a house.

14. **Close** ✖ the Clip Art task pane.

15. **Size** the clip art appropriately for the page.

16. Make sure the **image** is selected.

17. Choose **Format→Size→Crop** 🖼 from the Ribbon.

18. **Crop** the picture from both sides to remove any extra background area without removing the actual house.

19. Choose **Format→Picture Styles** from the Ribbon.

20. Choose a **Picture Style** from the gallery.

21. Choose **Format→Picture Styles→Picture Border** ✎ from the Ribbon.

22. Choose a **border color** from the gallery.

23. Turn **off** the formatting marks.

24. **Save** 🖫 your file in your Lesson 06 folder, and **close** it.

Edit a Picture

In this exercise, you will open a flier and add a picture to it and make editing changes to the picture.

1. **Open** rs-Bandelier from the Lesson 06 folder.

2. **Tap** [Ctrl] + [End] to position the insertion point at the end of the document.

3. Choose **Insert→Illustrations→Picture** 🖼 from the Ribbon.

4. **Insert** the rs-Bandelier Long House picture in your document. It's located in the Lesson 06 folder.

Change the Brightness and Contrast

5. Make sure the **picture** is selected.

6. Choose **Format→Adjust→Corrections** ☀ from the Ribbon.

7. Choose **Picture Correction Options** from the menu.

8. Use the spinner arrow next to **Brightness** to adjust to +40%.

9. Use the spinner arrow next to **Contrast** to adjust it to –40%; click the **Close** button.

10. Choose **Format→Adjust→Reset Picture** 🖼 from the Ribbon to set the picture at its original brightness and contrast.

Crop the Picture

11. Choose **Format→Size→Crop** 🖼 from the Ribbon.
    Notice the cropping handles (thick black lines) surrounding the picture.

12. Place the opening of the **Crop** tool over the top-center handle, and then **drag** to crop the top half of the photo so only a portion of the blue sky is visible in the upper-right corner.

13. Using the **top-right handle** on the photo, **drag** to the left so only the left side of the photo is visible.
    You can uncrop portions of a cropped picture at any time.

14. Use the **Crop** 🖼 tool to uncrop the picture back to its original proportions.

15. Choose **Format→Size→Crop** 🖼 to put away the Crop tool.

Rotate the Photo

16. Make sure the **picture** is still selected, and then use the green **Rotate** handle at the top of the image to rotate the picture **90°** to the right.

17. Click the **Undo** ↺ button to return it to its original position.

Use Picture Styles

18. With the **picture** selected, choose **Format→Picture Styles** from the Ribbon.

19. Click the **More** ⏷ button on the Picture Styles gallery to display the entire gallery.

20. Choose the **sixth style** in the last row, Metal Rounded Rectangle. The actual location may vary in your gallery.

21. Make sure the **picture** is still selected.

22. Choose **Home→Paragraph→Center** ≡ from the Ribbon.

23. **Resize** the picture to your satisfaction.

24. **Save** 🖫 the file, and **close** it.

Apply Your Skills

Format a Two-Column Newsletter

In this exercise, you will open a document and convert the first heading line to WordArt. Then you will lay out the document in two columns, format the WordArt, and apply a Theme.

1. **Open** as-Conservation from your Lesson 06 folder.

2. If necessary, choose **Home→Paragraph→Show/Hide** ¶ from the Ribbon to display formatting marks.

3. Follow these guidelines to create your newsletter:

   ■ Convert the **first heading line** to WordArt style Fill - Blue, Accent 1, Metal Bevel, Reflection (fifth column, sixth row).

   ■ **Recolor** the WordArt object with the Shape Fill color of your choice.

   ■ Format the **next two heading lines** with center alignment, Cambria font, bold 12pt.

   ■ Insert a **continuous** section break to the left of the first heading in the body of the newsletter.

   ■ Set up a **two-column** layout in the second section.

   ■ Insert a **column** break to the left of the paragraph beginning *If your home is in....*

   ■ Apply the **Solstice Theme** to your newsletter.

   ■ Insert a **clip art image** of a frog, or another wetland creature of your choice, on the second blank line below the third heading line. Size the image appropriately for the page. Center the image, and rotate it to your satisfaction.

   ■ Insert **dropped caps** to the first letter of the three paragraph headings.

   Hint: You may need to resize the frog image again to make the columns break appropriately.

   ■ Turn **off** the formatting marks.

   ■ **Save** 💾 the file, and then **close** it.

Create Custom Building Blocks

In this exercise, you will create custom Building Blocks out of text, a clip art image, and a WordArt object.

1. **Open** as-Quick Parts from your Lesson 06 folder.

2. **Save** each of the items in the document (text, clip art, and WordArt) as three separate **Building Blocks**.

3. Leave the **inside address** Building Block name as Bailey, Stevens.

4. Name the **clip art** Building Block **Building Clip**.

5. Name the **WordArt** Building Block **Bailey WordArt**.

6. Start a **new** blank document, where you will create a letterhead for the firm Bailey, Stevens, and Sheppard.

7. **Insert** your Building Blocks into the document in this order: Bailey WordArt, Building Clip, Bailey, Stevens. Place each Building Block on a separate line, and add space between Building Blocks as you deem appropriate.

8. **Size** the clip art as you wish and center align the items.

9. When you complete the letterhead, **delete** your custom Building Blocks from the Quick Parts menu.

10. **Save** your new document as **as-Bailey Letterhead** in your Lesson 06 folder, and then **close** it.

Critical Thinking & Work-Readiness Skills

In the course of working through the following Microsoft Office-based Critical Thinking exercises, you will also be utilizing various work-readiness skills, some of which are listed next to each exercise. Go to labyrinthelab.com/ workreadiness to learn more about the work-readiness skills.

6.1 Design a Newsletter

Jenna is tasked with designing and publishing a newsletter to keep everyone informed of important or motivational, fun developments regarding Green Clean. While the newsletter will often be viewed online, there will also be a printed edition available in break rooms and sent to important customers and prospects. Design a one-page newsletter with three columns, inserting column breaks as necessary. Include at least four newsletter items, such as President's Corner, Welcome New Customers, Customer Feedback, Birthday List, Department News, or your own creative ideas. Use at least one piece of decorative WordArt and at least two pieces of clip art. Wrap text around each. Be creative with the text or use placeholder "dummy" text. Save the file as **ct-Newsletter Design** to your Lesson 06 folder.

WORK-READINESS SKILLS APPLIED
- Serving clients/ customers
- Seeing things in the mind's eye
- Thinking creatively

6.2 Improve Your Newsletter

Jenna wants to spice up her newsletter a little before distributing it. If necessary, open the ct-Newsletter Design file you created in the previous exercise. Have a partner look at your newsletter and offer comments and suggestions for improvement, such as adjusting column widths, fonts, and colors. Make changes based on your partner's feedback. Add a preformatted text box to identify the month or issue number of the newsletter and save it as a Building Block you can use for future newsletters. Save your file as **ct-Newsletter Design2** in your Lesson 06 folder.

WORK-READINESS SKILLS APPLIED
- Taking responsibility
- Thinking creatively
- Participating as a member of a team

6.3 Use Themes, Drop Caps, and More in Your Newsletter

Open the ct-Newsletter Design2 file, if necessary, and save a copy of it to your Lesson 06 folder with the new name **ct-Newsletter Design Final**. Experiment with applying themes, including customized themes. Insert dropped caps at the beginning of each paragraph and see how you like it. Use zoom controls to help you get the look just right. Save your changes. How do these finishing touches help you convey the positive message the newsletter is supposed to convey? If working in a group, discuss this question. If working alone, type your answer in a Word document named **ct-Questions** saved to your Lesson 06 folder.

WORK-READINESS SKILLS APPLIED
- Thinking creatively
- Making decisions
- Serving clients/ customers

7

Creating a Manual and Using Mail Merge

LESSON OUTLINE

LEARNING OBJECTIVES

After studying this lesson, you will be able to:

- Format documents with styles
- Create custom styles
- Modify styles
- Control document margins
- Use helpful techniques for navigating and viewing documents
- Set up a Mail Merge document and labels

Word provides a variety of tools that are particularly suited to working with multipage documents. Styles offer a powerful means of ensuring formatting consistency throughout large documents. Special navigation features make it easy to move around long documents, and the Split and Arrange All views make it easy to work with long documents and multiple documents. In this lesson, you will work with these tools as you create an employee policy manual. You will also use Mail Merge to create a form letter to send to employees and set up mailing labels for envelopes.

Formatting and Distributing a Policy Manual

Jenna Mann is the administrative assistant for Green Clean, a successful, environmentally conscience janitorial service company. She has been tasked with the job of producing an employee policy manual to distribute to all Green Clean employees. Jenna's Microsoft Office expertise lets her take advantage of the variety of tools Word offers. She uses Word's built-in styles to format the manual's headings, thus ensuring consistent formatting throughout the document. If she decides to modify a style, Word automatically updates all text associated with that style. When she's finished with the policy manual, Jenna will use Mail Merge to insert the employee's name into a form letter and create mailing labels. Mail Merge will save Jenna many hours that she would have otherwise spent addressing each letter individually.

Purpose of This Manual

The purpose of this manual is to inform you about Green Clean's business practices, employment policies, and benefits provided to you as a valued Green Clean employee. No employee manual can answer every question, so you should feel free to ask questions of your supervisor. Also, feel free to contact the Human Resources department if you have any questions or concerns. It is our desire to keep an open line of communication between you and the company.

Notice

Green Clean reserves the right to modify, amend, and update the policies outlined in this manual at any time. No oral or written statement by a supervisor, manager, or department head may be interpreted as a change in policy, nor will it constitute an agreement with an employee. This manual represents the sole agreement with respect to benefits between the employee and Green Clean. If this manual is updated, you will be given replacement pages for those that have become outdated. A copy will also be placed on our intranet site.

Your Green Clean Benefits

You may not have thought about it, but the value of your benefits amounts to a considerable sum each year in addition to the salary you earn. These are just some of the benefits Green Clean provides to eligible employees each year:

Credit union membership
Dental insurance
Disability leave of absence
Education assistance
Employee assistance program
Group-term life insurance
Health insurance
Paid holidays
Paid vacations

Word 2010's Quick Styles gallery makes it easy to apply professional formatting to a document in mere seconds.

7.1 Formatting Text with Styles

Video Lesson labyrinthelab.com/videos

A *style* is one of the most powerful formatting tools in Word. A style is a group of formats identified by a unique style name, such as Heading 1. It enables you to rapidly apply multiple formats to a block of text. Styles not only create consistent formatting throughout a document, they allow you to make global formatting changes by modifying the style definition. When you modify a style, the changes are applied to all text formatted with that style.

TIP

Remember, anything that ends with a paragraph symbol is considered a paragraph. A heading line is considered a paragraph because it ends with a paragraph symbol.

Types of Styles

Word supports several kinds of styles, as discussed below.

- **Character styles**—Character styles are applied to the word the insertion point is in or to a selected group of words. Character styles can only contain character formats, not paragraph formats. You can apply character styles to text *within* a paragraph that is formatted with a paragraph style. The character style overrides the formats applied by the paragraph style.

- **Paragraph styles**—Paragraph styles are applied to all text in selected paragraphs or to the paragraph containing the insertion point. You can use any character or paragraph formats in a paragraph style. For example, you may want to format a heading with a large, bold font (character formatting) and apply paragraph spacing before and after the heading (paragraph formatting).

When you create a new style, whether it's a character or a paragraph style, you use the Create New Style from Formatting dialog box. A character style is being created in the following illustration.

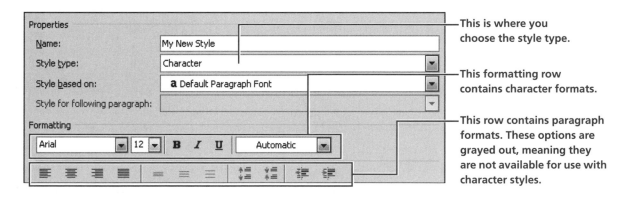

- **Linked styles**—Linked styles (paragraph and character) can behave as either character or paragraph styles. If you simply position the insertion point in a paragraph and apply a linked style, it formats the entire paragraph. If you select a word or several words first, and then apply the style, it applies only to the selected words.

- **List styles**—This feature makes it easy to convert text to a list and to ensure consistency among multiple lists in a document.

- **Table styles**—Table styles can provide consistent formats for multiple tables within a document.

The Normal Style

You are always working within a style in Word. The default style for Word is the *Normal* style. It contains the default formatting that you are familiar with, such as the default Calibri font, the 1.15 line spacing, and so forth.

Quick Styles

Word's Quick Styles gallery contains a group of styles designed to complement each other, and they are based on the current document theme. The gallery contains styles for headings, titles, lists, and special character formatting. Live Preview makes it easy to test a variety of styles in your document before you actually apply the style. The Quick Styles gallery is in the Styles group on the Home tab. When you use a style from the gallery, it then becomes visible in the gallery on the Ribbon without scrolling or opening the gallery. This makes it convenient should you wish to apply the same style several times in a row.

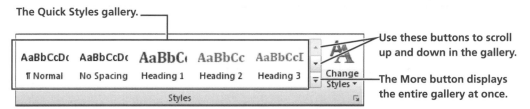

The Quick Styles gallery.

Use these buttons to scroll up and down in the gallery.

The More button displays the entire gallery at once.

The Quick Styles gallery does not contain all of Word's built-in styles. There are many more styles available, as you will see later in this lesson.

DEVELOP YOUR SKILLS 7.1.1
Preview Quick Styles

In this exercise, you will open a document that contains the content for Green Clean's employee policy manual. Then you will use Live Preview and Quick Styles to decide on the styles you wish to use to give the manual a professional, polished look.

1. Start **Word**, and make sure the Word window is **maximized** 🔲.

2. **Open** the Employee Policy Manual document from your Lesson 07 folder.
   This document uses Word's default formatting, with the exception of headings, which are bolded to make them easy to locate.

3. Position the **insertion point** in the first line of the document.

4. Follow these steps to examine the Quick Styles gallery in the **Home→Styles** group on the Ribbon:

Ⓐ **Scroll down** row-by-row through the gallery. (This is tedious, and makes it difficult to get an idea of all the styles available.)

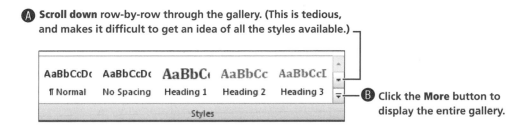

Ⓑ Click the **More** button to display the entire gallery.

5. Hover the **mouse pointer** over the Heading 1, Heading 2, and Title styles to see the Live Preview effect.
One of these styles would be appropriate for the first main heading in the document.

6. Hover the **mouse pointer** over some of the other styles.
You can tell which styles are strictly character (versus paragraph) styles. During Live Preview, they only affect the word where the insertion point is located. With character styles, if you intend to format more than one word, you must select the words prior to applying the style.

Apply the Title Style

7. Click the **Title** style to apply it to the heading.

8. Position the **insertion point** in the next heading line, *You're Part of Our Team.*

Apply Heading 1 and Heading 2 Styles

9. Follow these steps to apply a Heading 1 style to the selected heading:

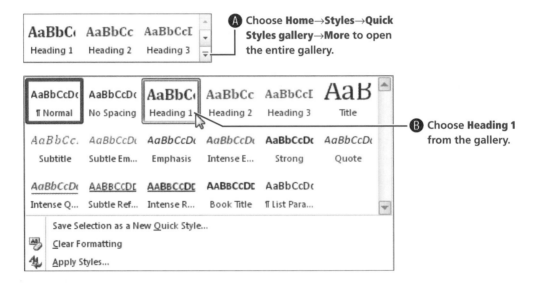

10. Apply **Heading 1** to the other bolded headings on page 1.

11. **Scroll** to the top of the second page, place the **insertion point** in the first heading, and apply the **Heading 1 style**.

12. Position the **insertion point** in the next heading line *Notice*, and apply the **Heading 2** style from the gallery.

13. Apply **Heading 1** to the next heading, *Your Green Clean Benefits.*

Convert Text to a List Style

14. On the **second page**, select the benefits from *Credit union membership* through *Paid vacations.*

15. Open the gallery, and choose the **List Paragraph** style—the last one in the gallery.
Notice that the List Paragraph style is now visible in the gallery on the Ribbon without scrolling or opening the gallery.

16. For each of the next three pages, apply the **Heading 1** style to the first heading on the page and the **Heading 2** style to the remaining headings on the page.

17. Save the file and leave it **open**; you will use it throughout the rest of the lesson.

Viewing All Styles

Video Lesson   labyrinthelab.com/videos

Clicking the dialog box launcher ⬐ in the bottom-right corner of the Styles group displays the Styles task pane. It lists all the styles present in the current Quick Styles gallery.

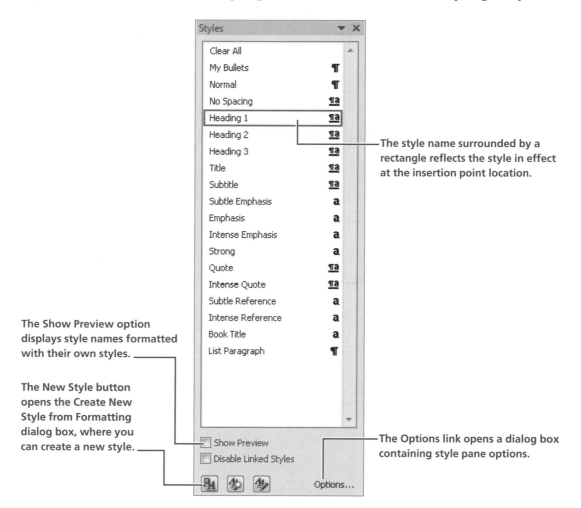

The style name surrounded by a rectangle reflects the style in effect at the insertion point location.

The Show Preview option displays style names formatted with their own styles.

The New Style button opens the Create New Style from Formatting dialog box, where you can create a new style.

The Options link opens a dialog box containing style pane options.

Reveal Style Formatting

To see all of the formats involved in a style, hover the mouse pointer over the style name in the Styles pane, and a pop-up menu appears, describing the font and paragraph formatting contained in the style.

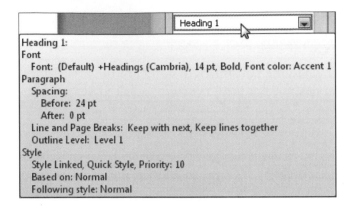

Changing the Quick Style Set

Word comes with a variety of Quick Style sets that you can display in the Quick Styles gallery. This enhances the array of styles available directly from the Ribbon. All of the styles in a set are coordinated to work together. Selecting a new style set affects only the current document you are viewing. If you switch to a different open document, the style set chosen for that document will display.

When you click the Change Styles button in the Styles group, Word displays a menu from which you can choose the Style Set command to display a submenu of Word's built-in sets.

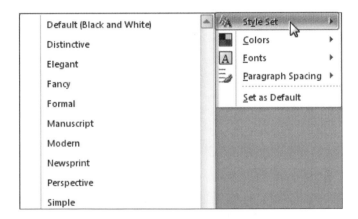

DEVELOP YOUR SKILLS 7.1.2
Change the Style Set

In this exercise, you will explore Word's style sets and apply a new style set.

1. **Scroll** to the top of the document.

2. Choose **Home→Styles→Change Styles** from the Ribbon.

3. Follow these steps to choose a new style set:

Ⓐ Click **Style Set** from the menu to display the style sets.

Ⓑ View the **Live Preview** of various style sets, and then click **Formal** to apply that style to the document.

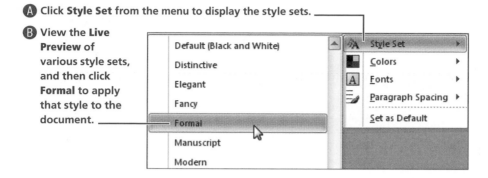

4. Scroll through the document to see the impact of the new style.

5. Open the **Quick Styles** gallery to see the formatting of the other styles in the **Formal** set.

6. Click in the document to close the gallery.

Apply the Word 2010 Style Set

7. Choose **Home→Styles→Change Styles** 🗚 from the Ribbon.

8. Choose **Style Set** from the menu, and then choose **Word 2010** from the submenu to return to the original look.

Creating a New Custom Style

Video Lesson labyrinthelab.com/videos

Thus far, you have applied built-in styles. However, there may be situations where the built-in styles do not meet your needs. For example, you may have corporate formatting standards set for different types of documents. You can create custom styles to meet those standards.

There are two approaches you can take to create custom styles. The method you choose is a matter of personal preference; both are equally effective.

- **Define a style by definition**—When creating a custom style in the Create New Style from Formatting dialog box, one option is to open the dialog box and choose all formats from within the dialog box.

- **Define a style by example**—The other option is to format a block of text with the formats you wish to include in your style. Then select the text, and when you open the dialog box, you will see that Word copies the formats from the selected text into the dialog box. At this point, you can make additional formatting selections if you wish.

Making Detailed Style Settings

Clicking the New Style 🗚 button at the bottom of the Styles task pane displays the Create New Style from Formatting dialog box. You can use this dialog box to set all of the formatting for a new style, or use it to tweak the formatting of a style you are creating from selected text. For example, after setting all the formatting to create a style by example, you may want to open this dialog box to choose the style for the following paragraph.

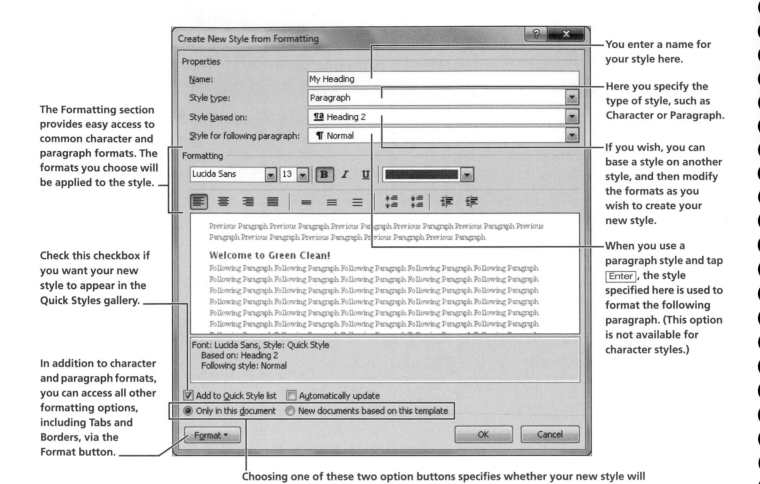

The Formatting section provides easy access to common character and paragraph formats. The formats you choose will be applied to the style.

You enter a name for your style here.

Here you specify the type of style, such as Character or Paragraph.

If you wish, you can base a style on another style, and then modify the formats as you wish to create your new style.

Check this checkbox if you want your new style to appear in the Quick Styles gallery.

When you use a paragraph style and tap Enter, the style specified here is used to format the following paragraph. (This option is not available for character styles.)

In addition to character and paragraph formats, you can access all other formatting options, including Tabs and Borders, via the Format button.

Choosing one of these two option buttons specifies whether your new style will be available in this document only or in all documents based on the current template. In our example, that is the default Normal template. This means your new style would be available in all new documents based on the Normal style.

DEVELOP YOUR SKILLS 7.1.3

Create a New Style

In this exercise, you will create a new character style and apply the style to selected blocks of text.

Create a Custom Style

1. On the **first page**, locate the heading *Green Clean Is Committed to Two Goals*.

2. In the first paragraph below the heading, **select** the words *best quality, eco-friendly products and services*.

3. Using the Mini toolbar, apply **Bold** **B** and **Underline** **U** to the selected text.

4. If necessary, choose **Home→Styles→dialog box launcher** 🔲 in the bottom-right corner of the Styles group on the Home tab to display the Styles task pane.

5. Click the **New Style** 🔢 button, the far left button at the bottom of the Styles task pane, to display the **Create New Style from Formatting** dialog box.

6. Follow these steps to complete the new style by definition:

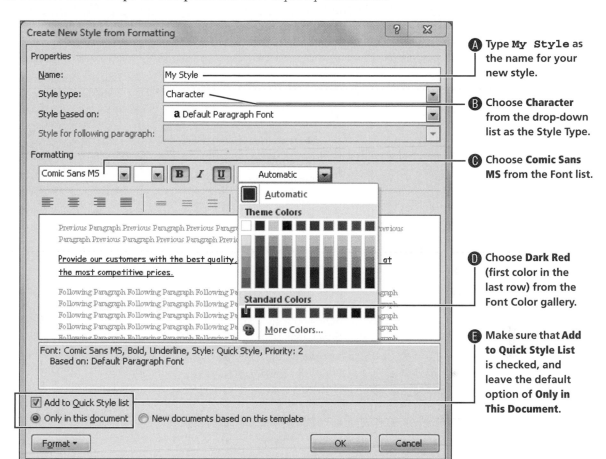

7. Click **OK** to finish creating the style and to apply it to the selected text.

Apply Your New Style

8. **Select** the words *above average compensation* in the next paragraph.

9. In the Quick Styles gallery, click your new **My Style** to apply it to the selected text.

10. **Click** anywhere in the document to deselect the text.

11. **Save** 💾 your file, and continue with the next topic.

Modifying, Removing, and Deleting Styles

Video Lesson labyrinthelab.com/videos

You can modify built-in styles as well as styles that you create. The ability to modify styles is one of the great powers of Word. Imagine, for example, that you used a heading style that contained a font change, point size change, font color change, bold, and italic, and you applied that style to twenty headings in a long document. Later you decide that you don't like the italic formatting. Rather than going to all twenty headings and removing italics, just modify the style, and all text with that style applied will update immediately.

You can remove a style from the Quick Styles gallery without removing it from the Styles task pane. You can leave it in the task pane for future use, or if you prefer you can delete it from the task pane. Take a moment to examine several of the commands in a style's menu in the Styles task pane.

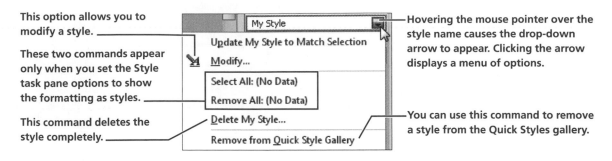

This option allows you to modify a style.

These two commands appear only when you set the Style task pane options to show the formatting as styles.

This command deletes the style completely.

Hovering the mouse pointer over the style name causes the drop-down arrow to appear. Clicking the arrow displays a menu of options.

You can use this command to remove a style from the Quick Styles gallery.

QUICK REFERENCE	USING WORD STYLES
Task	**Procedure**
Apply a style	▪ Apply a character style by selecting the words to be formatted and then choosing a style from the Quick Styles gallery on the Home tab or from the Styles task pane.
	▪ Apply a paragraph style by clicking in the paragraph and then choosing a style from the Quick Styles gallery on the Home tab or from the Styles task pane. If you want to apply a style to more than one paragraph at a time, you must select the paragraphs.
Create a new style by definition	▪ Click the New Style button at the bottom of the Styles task pane to open the Create New Style from Formatting dialog box.
	▪ Choose all desired formats from within the dialog box.
Create a new style by example	▪ Format a block of text with the desired formats.
	▪ Click the New Style button at the bottom of the Styles task pane to open the Create New Style from Formatting dialog box. Word copies the formats from the block of formatted text.
	▪ You can make additional format changes within the dialog box if you wish.
Modify a style	▪ In the Styles task pane, hover the mouse pointer over the style to be modified.
	▪ When the drop-down arrow appears, click it to display the menu.
	▪ Choose Modify from the menu to display the Modify Style dialog box.
Add a style to the Quick Styles gallery	▪ In the Styles task pane, hover the mouse pointer over the style to be added.
	▪ When the drop-down arrow appears, click it to display the menu.
	▪ Choose Add to Quick Style Gallery from the menu.
Remove a style from the Quick Styles gallery	▪ In the Styles task pane, hover the mouse pointer over the style to be removed.
	▪ When the drop-down arrow appears, click it to display the menu.
	▪ Choose Remove from Quick Style Gallery from the menu.
Delete a custom style	▪ In the Styles task pane, hover the mouse pointer over the style to be deleted.
	▪ When the drop-down arrow appears, click it to display the menu.
	▪ Choose Delete [style name] from the menu.

Modify and Remove a Quick Styles

In this exercise, you will modify a style to see how it impacts all text formatted with that style. Then you will remove the style from the Quick Styles gallery. The Styles task pane should still be open.

1. Hover the **mouse pointer** over My Style in the Styles task pane to display the drop-down arrow.

2. **Click** the arrow to display the menu.

3. Choose the **Modify** command from the menu to open the Modify Style dialog box.
   This dialog box contains the same elements as the Create New Style from Formatting dialog box.

4. Click the **Italic** button to add italic formatting to the style.

5. Click **OK** and notice that both blocks of text formatted with My Style updated with the modification.

Remove a Style from the Quick Styles Gallery

6. In the Styles task pane, click the drop-down arrow for **My Style** again to display the menu.

7. Choose **Remove from Quick Styles Gallery** from the menu.
   Notice that removing the style from the Quick Styles gallery does not remove the formatting from the text with that style.

8. Open the **Quick Styles** gallery, and notice that your new style no longer appears in the gallery.

9. **Click** in the document to close the gallery.

Delete a Style from the Styles Task Pane

10. Display the **My Style** menu in the Styles task pane again.

11. Choose **Delete My Style** from the menu.

12. When the message appears verifying that you want to delete the style, click **Yes**.
    Notice that the My Style formatting has been removed from the two blocks of text in the document, and that My Style no longer appears in the Styles task pane.

13. Click the **Close** ☒ button in the upper-right corner of the Styles task pane.

14. **Save** 🖫 your file, and leave it **open** for the next topic.

7.2 Navigating with the Navigation Pane

Video Lesson   labyrinthelab.com/videos

One of the options in the new Navigation pane is to use the Browse the Headings in your Document button to maneuver around in a document quickly. This option is activated only when you have assigned Heading styles to text. To do so, open the Navigation pane from the Editing group on the Home tab of the Ribbon.

Rearranging Sections

Rearranging sections is one of the most powerful uses of the Navigation pane. When you create a document, you may decide to change the order of topics later. Although you could use the Cut and Paste method to rearrange the document, using the Navigation pane is much easier because you can drag the headings up and down the pane to reposition them. When you drag a heading to a new location, all of its lower-level headings and paragraph text move right along with it. For example, you may have a Heading 1 followed by a paragraph, followed by a Heading 2 with its own paragraph. When you move the Heading 1, Word also moves the Heading 1 paragraph, the Heading 2, and the Heading 2 paragraph all as one section.

QUICK REFERENCE	REARRANGING A DOCUMENT USING THE NAVIGATION PANE
Task	**Procedure**
Display headings in the Navigation pane	■ Choose Home→Editing→Find from the Ribbon to open the Navigation pane. ■ Click the Browse the Headings in Your Document button in the Navigation pane.
Rearrange a section	■ Click and drag a heading in the Navigation pane up or down to a new location.

DEVELOP YOUR SKILLS 7.2.1
Rearrange a Document Using the Navigation Pane

In this exercise, you will rearrange the order of sections in a document by dragging headings in the Navigation pane.

1. Choose **Home→Editing→Find** from the Ribbon to open the Navigation pane.

2. Click the **Browse the Headings in Your Document** tab to display the text that is formatted as headings.

3. Follow these steps to move the Employment Classifications section above the Employment Policies section:

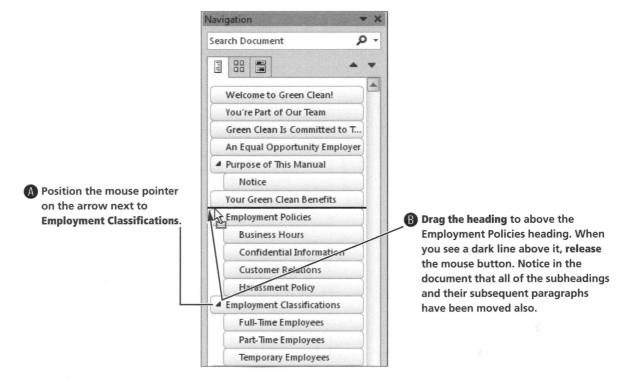

Ⓐ Position the mouse pointer on the arrow next to **Employment Classifications**.

Ⓑ **Drag the heading** to above the Employment Policies heading. When you see a dark line above it, **release** the mouse button. Notice in the document that all of the subheadings and their subsequent paragraphs have been moved also.

4. Scroll through the document to see changes.

5. Using the same technique, **move** the *Employment Policies* heading back above the *Employment Classifications* section.

6. Tap Ctrl + Home to position the insertion point at the top, then close ☒ the Navigation Pane.

7. Save 💾 the file and leave it **open** for the next exercise.

7.3 Changing Word Window Views

Video Lesson labyrinthelab.com/videos

Word provides many different ways of viewing your documents on the screen. The Arrange All command arranges all open Word documents on the screen. Initially, it displays the windows horizontally, one above the other. You can also view the two windows side-by-side vertically. Whichever view the two documents are in, you can choose to scroll through them separately or simultaneously. You might use this view with the synchronous scrolling option to compare two versions of a document, as an example. The Split command splits a document's window into two individual windows that you can scroll separately. This provides the ability to compare two different parts of the same document next to each other.

QUICK REFERENCE	WORKING WITH WORD WINDOW VIEWS
View	**Procedure**
Arrange All	Choose View→Window→Arrange All from the Ribbon.
View Side by Side	Choose View→Window→View Side by Side from the Ribbon.
Split	Choose View→Window→Split from the Ribbon.

How the Split Bar Works

When you choose View→Window→Split ▭ from the Ribbon, Word displays the split bar, which spans the width of the window. The mouse pointer looks like a double-headed arrow.

The split bar moves when you move the mouse. You position the mouse pointer where you want the split bar on the screen, and then click the mouse button to anchor the bar.

DEVELOP YOUR SKILLS 7.3.1
Use the View Side By Side and Split Views

In this exercise, you will use the View Side by Side command to display both open Word documents at the same time and scroll through both documents at the same time. Finally, you will use the Split command to split your Employee Policy Manual into two windows, which you can scroll separately.

Use the View Side By Side View

1. **Open** the Original Employee Policy Manual document from the Lesson 07 folder.

2. Choose **View→Window→View Side by Side** 📖 from the Ribbon.
   The documents now appear next to each other in separate windows. Each window has its own scroll bar.

3. **Scroll down** and then back **up** to the top using the scroll bar on the Original Employee Policy Manual.
   These are actually two separate files, each with its own title bar, Ribbon, and scroll bar. Notice that both documents scroll simultaneously instead of separately.

4. Choose **View→Window→Synchronous Scrolling** 🔃 from the Ribbon on the Original Employee Policy Manual.

5. Take a moment to **scroll** through each window.
   Notice that each window scrolls independently from the other.

6. Click the **Close** ![X] button in the upper-right corner of the Original Employee Policy Manual document to close it.

7. If necessary, **maximize** ![□] the Employee Policy Manual window.

Split the Document Window

8. Choose **View→Window→Split** ![icon] from the Ribbon.
   Word displays the split bar, which horizontally spans the width of the window. The mouse pointer appears as a double-headed arrow attached to the split bar.

9. Drag the **mouse pointer** up and down to change the position of the split bar.

10. Move the **split bar** to the center of the screen, and click to anchor the bar.

You can place the mouse pointer on the split bar at any time and drag to reposition it.

   Notice that each part of the split window has its own scroll bar.

11. Take a moment to **scroll** both sections of the window independently.
    Splits are handy for positioning separate parts of the same document next to each other for comparison purposes.

    Notice that the Split command on the Ribbon changed to Remove Split.

12. Choose **View→Window→Remove Split** ![icon] to put the split bar away.

13. **Save** ![icon] your file, and **close** it.

7.4 Introducing Mail Merge

Video Lesson   labyrinthelab.com/videos

Word's Mail Merge feature is most often used for generating personalized form letters, mailing labels, and envelopes. However, Mail Merge is a versatile tool that can be used with any type of document. Mail Merge can be a big time-saver and is invaluable for managing large mailings. When you perform a merge, you have the option to merge directly to a printer or to a new document.

Components of a Mail Merge

Merging creates a merged document by combining information from two or more documents. The documents are known as the *main document* and the *data source*.

■ **Main Document**—This document controls the merge. It contains the fixed information into which the variable information for each contact is merged. In a typical form letter, for instance, you will have a different name and address on each letter, while the rest of the text is the same for everyone receiving the letter.

Remember that whatever text is to be included in every letter should be typed in the main document.

- **Data Source**—This can be another Word document, a spreadsheet, a database file, or a contacts list in Outlook. When creating the data source, keep in mind how you want to use the data in the merge. For example, if you want the letter to be addressed informally using the first names, then in the data source, there must be a separate column (field) for the first name.

- **Merged Document**—This document is the result after you perform the merge. It contains all of the individual letters addressed to each individual in the data source you used. You can save this document, if you wish, or simply close it without saving after you print.

You can merge an existing main document with an existing data source, or you can create the main document and data source while stepping through the merge process.

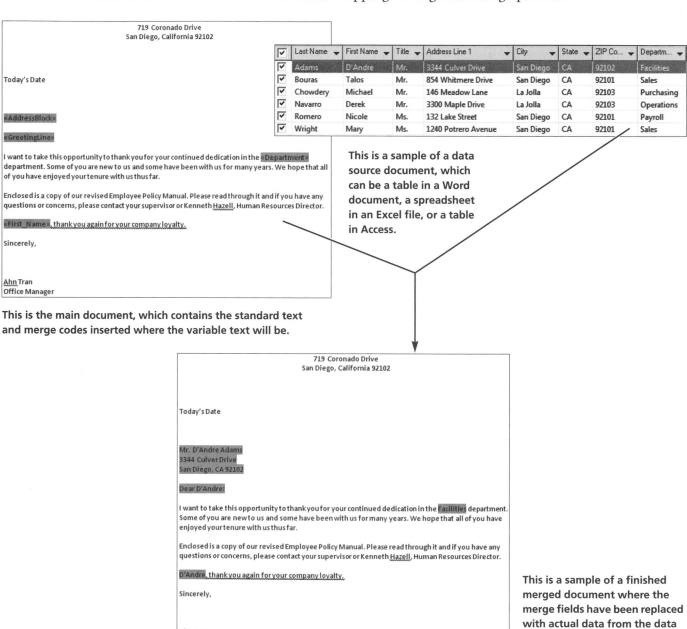

This is the main document, which contains the standard text and merge codes inserted where the variable text will be.

This is a sample of a data source document, which can be a table in a Word document, a spreadsheet in an Excel file, or a table in Access.

This is a sample of a finished merged document where the merge fields have been replaced with actual data from the data source document.

The Benefits of Using Mail Merge

Mail Merge will save you a lot of time and can help reduce errors in large mailings. For example, say you want to send a letter to 100 customers. Without using Mail Merge, you would be typing the same text in all 100 letters (or copying and pasting 100 times). However, using Mail Merge for the job, you create only one main document containing the standard text and one data source document containing the 100 customer names. You will also really appreciate Mail Merge when you later decide you want to make a change. Using Mail Merge, you can edit the main document once and remerge it with the data source to produce a new merged document. Without Mail Merge, you would need to edit each personalized letter individually.

The Mailings Tab

The Mailings tab on the Ribbon provides guidance in setting up both the main document and data source and helps you conduct the merge. The Start Mail Merge command group on the Mailings tab is the beginning point. Alternatively, you can choose Step by Step Mail Merge Wizard from the Start Mail Merge command to walk you through the process of choosing the main document, the data source document, inserting merge fields, and finally conducting the merge.

The Start Mail Merge command is where you specify the type of main document you want to use, such as letters, envelopes, or labels.

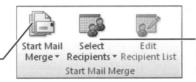

Select Recipients is where you either identify an existing data source list or create a new data source.

 The Mail Merge Wizard will be familiar to those who have conducted merges in earlier versions of Word.

7.5 Working with the Data Source

Video Lesson labyrinthelab.com/videos

Data sources usually contain names, addresses, telephone numbers, and other contact information. However, you can include any information in a data source. For example, you may want to include inventory names, numbers, and prices of parts, if you are using Mail Merge to create a parts catalog. You can create a data source in Word, or you can use external data sources, such as an Access database or an Excel worksheet. Once a data source is created, it can be used as a source for many different main documents.

Designing Effective Data Sources

It is very important that you design effective data sources. The most important consideration is the number of fields to use. The more fields, the more flexibility you will have in the merge. An important rule to remember is that you cannot merge a portion of a field. For example, if a field contains both a first name and last name, then you will never be able to merge only the last name into a main document. This would be a problem if you needed to merge only a last name to create salutations such as Dear Ms. Alvarez. In this example, you would need to use one field for the first name and a separate field for the last name. You would also need to use a title field for the titles Mr., Ms., and Mrs.

Creating Address Lists

You can use the New Address List dialog box to set up address lists (data sources) for use in mail merges. This tool stores the addresses you enter in a table within a Microsoft Access database. This table, which becomes the data source for the merge, is linked to the mail merge main document. You can also use a Word table, an Excel worksheet, or an Access table as a data source for a mail merge. Each of these tools stores data in a table or worksheet structure.

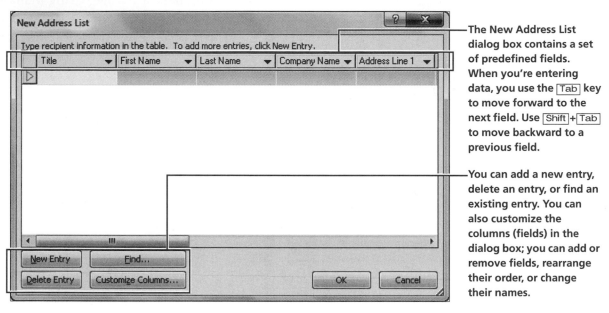

The New Address List dialog box contains a set of predefined fields. When you're entering data, you use the [Tab] key to move forward to the next field. Use [Shift]+[Tab] to move backward to a previous field.

You can add a new entry, delete an entry, or find an existing entry. You can also customize the columns (fields) in the dialog box; you can add or remove fields, rearrange their order, or change their names.

NOTE The terms *fields* and *columns* are used interchangeably in this lesson. Each row of data is referred to as a *record*.

Customizing an Address List

The Customize Address List dialog box makes it easy to set up the mailing list just as you want it. You can easily delete unnecessary fields and add your own custom fields to the list. You can also rename an existing field name and use the Move Up and Move Down buttons to reorder the list of fields.

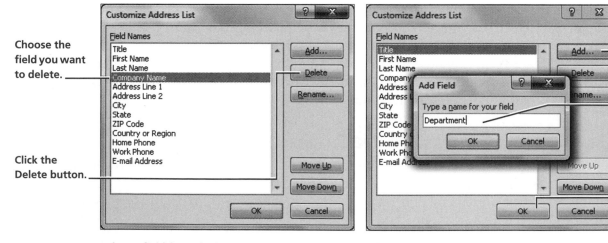

Choose the field you want to delete.

Click the Delete button.

Delete a field from the list.

Click the Add button.

Type the new field name in the Add Field dialog box.

Click OK to add the new custom field.

Add a field to the list.

Specify the Main Document and Create a Data Source

In this exercise, you will use the Start Mail Merge group on the Mailings tab to specify a letter as your main document, to customize the data source, and to enter data.

1. **Open** the Policy Manual Letter Main from the Lesson 07 folder.

2. Choose **Mailings→Start Mail Merge→Start Mail Merge** 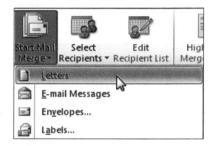 from the Ribbon.

3. Choose **Letters** from the menu, as shown at right.
   You are indicating here that the open document on the screen will be the main document.

Connect to the Data Source

Next you will indicate which data source will be connected to the letter. Since you don't have an existing data source, you will create one during the mail merge process.

4. Choose **Mailings→Start Mail Merge→Select Recipients** from the Ribbon.

5. Choose **Type New List** from the menu.

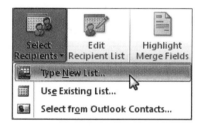

The New Address List dialog box opens.

Remove Fields

You will remove unnecessary fields from the set of predefined fields.

6. Click the **Customize Columns** button in the bottom-left corner of the dialog box to display the Customize Address List dialog box.

7. Choose the **Company Name** field.

8. Click the **Delete** button, and then click **Yes** when the message appears to verify the deletion.

9. **Delete** the Address Line 2, Country or Region, Home Phone, Work Phone, and E-mail Address fields; then, click on the **Title** field name at the top of the list.

Add a Field

10. Follow these steps to add a Department field to the list:

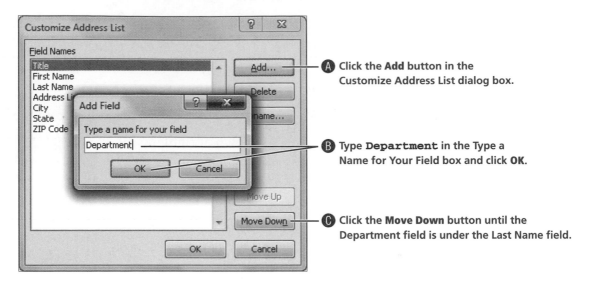

(A) Click the **Add** button in the Customize Address List dialog box.

(B) Type **Department** in the Type a Name for Your Field box and click **OK**.

(C) Click the **Move Down** button until the Department field is under the Last Name field.

11. Click **OK** to complete the changes.

Enter the First Record

The cursor should be in the Title field.

12. Type **Mr.**, and then **tap** Tab to move to the next field.

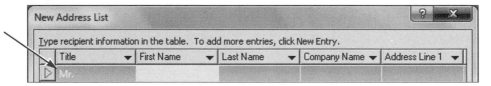

Do not type spaces after entering information in fields. Word will take care of adding the necessary spaces in the inside address and the salutation. You can always click in a field and make editing changes if necessary.

13. Type **Talos**, and then **tap** Tab to move to the next field.

14. Type **Bouras**, and then **tap** Tab to move to the next field.

15. Finish **entering** the Talos Bouras data shown in the following table, **tabbing** between fields. The list of fields will scroll as you continue to Tab and type.

16. When you complete the first record, click the **New Entry** button or **tap** Tab to generate a new blank row for the next record, and then **enter** the two remaining records shown in this table.

Mr. Talos Bouras	Ms. Nicole Romero	Mr. Michael Chowdery
Sales	Payroll	Purchasing
854 Whitmore Drive	132 Lake Street	900 C Street
San Diego, CA 92101	San Diego, CA 92101	La Jolla, CA 92103

If you accidentally tap Tab after the last record and add a blank record, just click the Delete Entry button.

17. Leave the New Address List dialog box **open**.

Reviewing Your Records

Video Lesson   labyrinthelab.com/videos

It's a good idea to review your records for accuracy before saving the data source. However, if you miss an error, you can always edit it in the Edit Data Source dialog box, which you'll learn about later in this lesson.

If an entry is wider than the default field width, you can click the insertion point directly in the field and use the arrow keys to move through the entry.

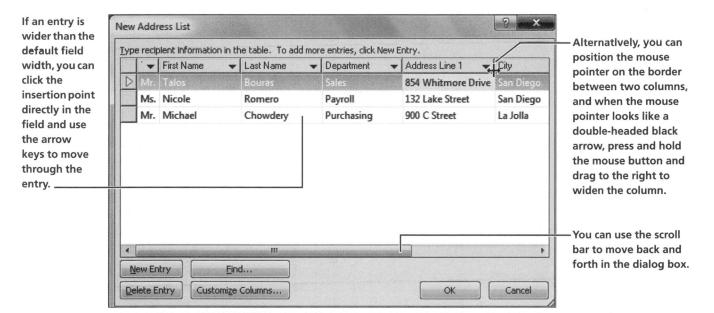

Alternatively, you can position the mouse pointer on the border between two columns, and when the mouse pointer looks like a double-headed black arrow, press and hold the mouse button and drag to the right to widen the column.

You can use the scroll bar to move back and forth in the dialog box.

DEVELOP YOUR SKILLS 7.5.2
Review and Save Your Work

In this exercise, you will take a moment to examine your records for accuracy, and then you will save your data source.

1. Position the **mouse pointer** on the scroll bar and drag left and right to view all the fields.

2. Click the **insertion point** in the Address Line 1 field for the first record, and use the **arrow keys** on the keyboard to move the insertion point through the entry.

3. Position the **mouse pointer** on the border between the Address Line 1 and City fields, and when the mouse pointer changes to a double-headed black arrow, **drag** to the **right** to display the entire *854 Whitmere Drive* entry.

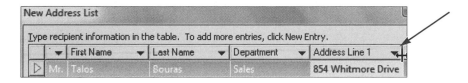

4. Make any needed revisions.

5. When you finish reviewing your records, click **OK** to open the Save Address List dialog box.

6. **Save** the data source file as **Policy Manual Letter Data** in the Lesson 07 folder. *Your data source is now connected to the main document.*

7. Leave the current document **open**, and stay in the Mailings tab on the Ribbon for the next exercise.

Managing the Address List

Video Lesson   labyrinthelab.com/videos

The Mail Merge Recipients dialog box lets you sort and filter address lists and choose records to include in a mail merge. To edit data, you click the Edit button in the Mail Merge Recipients dialog box to display the Edit Data Source dialog box, where you can add, delete, and edit entries.

 If you used a Word table, Excel spreadsheet, or other document for your data source, you can edit directly in that data source document if you wish. Since the data source is connected to the main document, any changes made are updated automatically in the main document.

You choose→Mailings→Start Mail Merge→Edit Recipient List ⊞ from the Ribbon to access the Mail Merge Recipients dialog box.

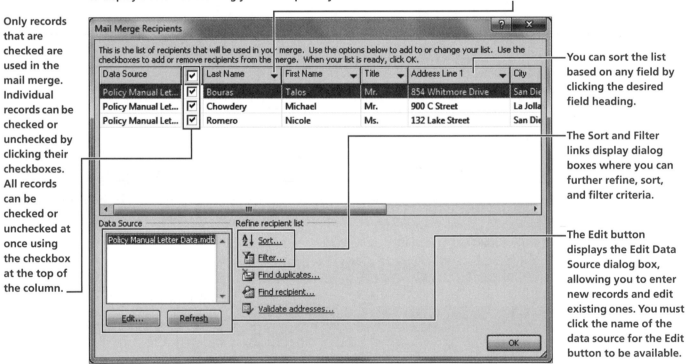

If there are records that you do not want to include in your mailing, use the menu ▼ buttons to display a filter list allowing you to temporarily hide records based on filter criteria.

Only records that are checked are used in the mail merge. Individual records can be checked or unchecked by clicking their checkboxes. All records can be checked or unchecked at once using the checkbox at the top of the column.

You can sort the list based on any field by clicking the desired field heading.

The Sort and Filter links display dialog boxes where you can further refine, sort, and filter criteria.

The Edit button displays the Edit Data Source dialog box, allowing you to enter new records and edit existing ones. You must click the name of the data source for the Edit button to be available.

The Edit Data Source dialog box looks and operates like the New Address List dialog box that you used to enter the original list.

Use Mail Merge Recipient Options and Edit Records

In this exercise, you will work with the Mail Merge Recipients dialog box, where you can sort, filter, and edit your mailing list.

1. Choose **Mailings→Start Mail Merge→Edit Recipient List** 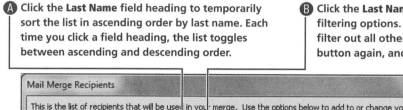 from the Ribbon.

2. Follow these steps to sort and filter the list and open the Edit Data Source dialog box:

Ⓐ Click the **Last Name** field heading to temporarily sort the list in ascending order by last name. Each time you click a field heading, the list toggles between ascending and descending order.

Ⓑ Click the **Last Name menu** ▼ button and notice the filtering options. Choose **Chowdery** from the menu to filter out all other entries. Click the **Last Name menu** ▼ button again, and choose **(All)** to redisplay all records.

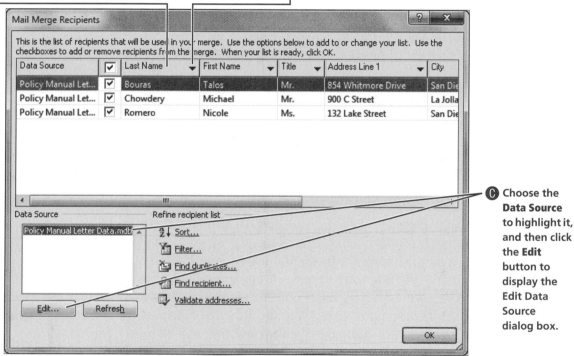

Ⓒ Choose the **Data Source** to highlight it, and then click the **Edit** button to display the Edit Data Source dialog box.

Edit a Record

Remember, the Edit Data Source dialog box looks and operates like the New Address List dialog box.

3. **Click** the *900 C Street* to highlight the text.

4. Type **146 Meadow Lane** in its place.

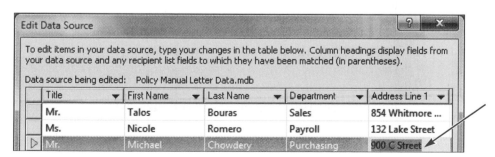

Add Recipients

5. Follow these guidelines to enter the three records at right:

Ms. Mary Wright	Mr. Derek Navarro	Mr. D'Andre Adams
Sales	Operations	3344 Culver Drive
1240 Potrero Avenue	3300 Maple Drive	San Diego, CA 92102
San Diego, CA 92101	La Jolla, CA 92103	

   ■ Use the **New Entry** button or **tap** Tab for each new record.

   ■ **Tap** Tab to move from one field to the next.

   ■ Notice that the third record does not include a department name. **Tap** Tab to pass through the department field and leave it empty.

   ■ Make sure to **enter** the data in the correct fields.

6. Click **OK** to close the dialog box.

7. Click **Yes** when the message appears verifying your update, and then notice your changes in the Mail Merge Recipients dialog box.
   Notice that Word remembers that you wanted the list sorted in alphabetical order by last name.

8. Click **OK** to close the Mail Merge Recipients dialog box.
   You will create the main document in the next exercise.

7.6 Working with Main Documents

Video Lesson   labyrinthelab.com/videos

You accomplish a merge by combining a main document with a data source. Typical main documents include form letters, envelopes, and mailing labels. A main document is linked to a data source that includes one or more merge fields. Merge fields inserted into a main document correspond to fields in the attached data source. Some merge fields, such as the address block, are composite fields consisting of a number of fields grouped together. For example, Title, First Name, Last Name, Address, City, State, and Zip would be included in the address block merge field.

Though not a necessity, including the word "main" in the document's name can be helpful in the future.

When you conduct a merge, a customized letter, envelope, or label is created for each record in the data source. After the merge is complete, you can save or print the merged document. The following figure shows the command buttons in the Write & Insert Fields group of the Mailings tab that you will use to insert merge fields into your letter.

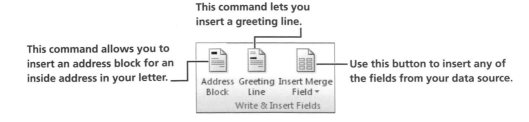

This command lets you insert a greeting line.

This command allows you to insert an address block for an inside address in your letter.

Use this button to insert any of the fields from your data source.

The following illustration shows the form letter with the location of the merge fields you will insert.

```
                              719 Coronado Drive
                           San Diego, California 92102




Today's Date


«AddressBlock»

«GreetingLine»

I want to take this opportunity to thank you for your continued dedication in the «Department»
department. Some of you are new to us and some have been with us for many years. We hope that all
of you have enjoyed your tenure with us thus far.

Enclosed is a copy of our revised Employee Policy Manual. Please read through it and if you have any
questions or concerns, please contact your supervisor or Kenneth Hazell, Human Resources Director.

 Thank you again for your company loyalty «First_Name».

Sincerely,




Ahn Tran
Office Manager

XX
```

When you execute the merge, the main document and data source are merged; the address block, greeting line, and merge fields are replaced with data from the data source.

Setting Up Main Documents

You can use any document as a mail merge main document. A document becomes a main document when you attach it to a data source and insert merge fields. In this lesson, you create a main document from the Policy Manual Letter Main document that is already open on your screen. Once a data source is attached, you can insert merge fields.

DEVELOP YOUR SKILLS 7.6.1

Set Up a Form Letter

In this exercise, you will set up a form letter. The Policy Manual Letter Main document should still be open.

1. If necessary, choose **Home→Paragraph→Show/Hide** ¶ from the Ribbon to display formatting characters.

Insert the Date

2. Using the left margin area, select the **Today's Date** line, and then **tap** Delete .

3. Choose **Insert→Text→Insert Date and Time** 🔲 from the Ribbon to display the Date and Time dialog box.

4. Choose the **third date** format on the list, check the **Update Automatically** checkbox in the bottom-right corner of the dialog box, and then click **OK**.

Checking this option instructs Word to insert the current date when the letter file is opened on a later date. The date in your letter will always be the current date, which is a convenient option for form letters that you want to use again.

5. **Tap** Enter four times after inserting the date.

Insert the Address Block

6. Choose **Mailings→Write & Insert Fields→Address Block** from the Ribbon.

The Insert Address Block dialog box appears, allowing you to choose a format for the address block. Notice that the Preview window is displaying the address block format of the option that is highlighted at the left side of the dialog box.

7. Follow these steps to insert an Address Block merge code:

Ⓐ **Click** on the different formats for the recipient's name, viewing the changes in the Preview box, and then choose **Mr. Joshua Randall Jr.**

Ⓑ Preview the results of removing the checkmark from the Insert Postal Address checkbox, and then **click** it again to reinsert the merge code into the document.

Ⓒ Click **OK** to accept the Address Block options.

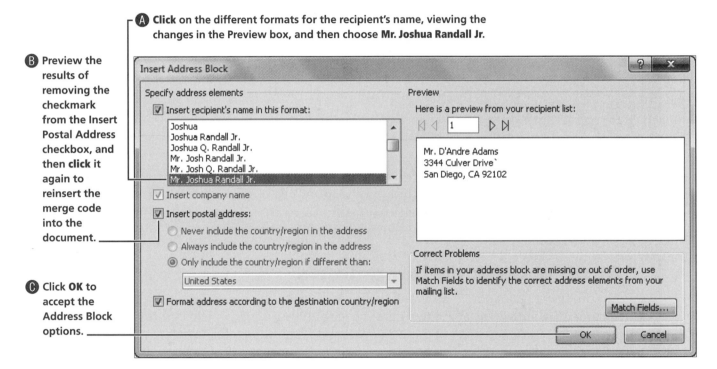

An Address Block merge code appears in the document. During the merge, Word inserts address information from the data source at the location in the customized letters.

8. **Tap** Enter twice.

Insert the Greeting Line

9. Choose **Mailings→Write & Insert Fields→Greeting Line** ![icon] from the Ribbon.

10. Follow these steps to modify and insert the greeting line:

A Click the **drop-down arrow** and change this option to a colon (:).

B Click the **drop-down arrow** and choose **Joshua** from the list.

C Notice that this style greeting will be used for the records in the data source if they are missing last names.

D Click **OK** to insert the greeting line code, and then **tap** Enter twice.

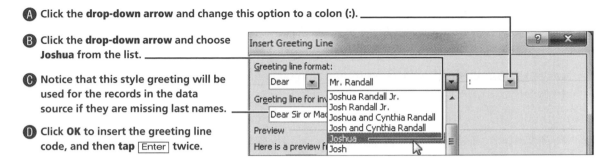

Insert Another Merge Field

11. Follow these steps to insert the Department merge field code into the letter:

A Position the **insertion point** at the end of the word *the* in the first line and tap Spacebar.

B Choose **Mailings→Write & Insert Fields→Insert Merge Field menu button** from the Ribbon to display a list of merge fields in the Data Source document.

C Choose **Department** from the merge field list.

12. Position the **insertion point** at the end of the line beginning with *Thank you again*.

13. Choose the **Mailings→Write & Insert Fields→** ![Insert Merge Field] menu button from the Ribbon.

14. Choose the **First_Name** field from the drop-down merge field list.

Review the Letter for Accuracy

15. Choose **Home→Paragraph→Show/Hide ¶** from the Ribbon to turn off the formatting marks.

16. Take a few moments to review your letter, making sure the merge fields match the preceding example. In particular, make sure you used the proper punctuation and spacing between fields and the text. Any punctuation or spacing errors that occur in your main document will appear in every merged letter.

17. Save 🖫 the letter in the Lesson 07 folder.

7.7 Conducting a Merge

Video Lesson labyrinthelab.com/videos

Merging combines a main document with a data source to produce a merged document. If you are merging a form letter with a data source, Word produces a personalized copy of the form letter for each record in the data source. You can print one or all of the records and save the merged document if you wish. It's always a good idea to preview what the document will look like when it is merged so you can make corrections to the main document, if needed.

Previewing the Results

The Preview Results group on the Mailings tab allows you to see how your letters will look before you complete the merge. If you notice an error that needs to be fixed in the main document, simply click the Preview Results button again to return to it.

Using Auto Check for Errors

When you have many records to preview, rather than previewing each one individually, you can use Auto Check for Errors. The feature goes through the document checking for common errors such as an invalid field code. In the Auto Check for Errors dialog box, you have three options for viewing errors:

- Simulate the merge and report errors in a new document
- Complete the merge, pausing to report each error as it occurs
- Complete the merge without pausing; errors are reported in a new document

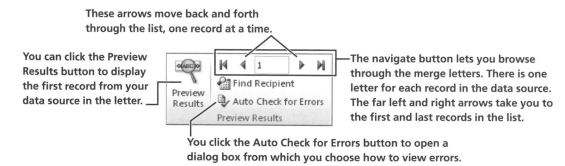

These arrows move back and forth through the list, one record at a time.

You can click the Preview Results button to display the first record from your data source in the letter.

The navigate button lets you browse through the merge letters. There is one letter for each record in the data source. The far left and right arrows take you to the first and last records in the list.

You click the Auto Check for Errors button to open a dialog box from which you choose how to view errors.

Finishing the Merge

When you feel confident that your letter and data source are accurate, you use the Finish & Merge command.

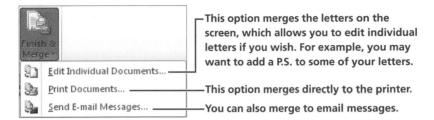

— This option merges the letters on the screen, which allows you to edit individual letters if you wish. For example, you may want to add a P.S. to some of your letters.

— This option merges directly to the printer.

— You can also merge to email messages.

To Save or Not to Save

Merged documents are rarely saved, because they can easily be reconstructed by merging the main document with the data source. A merged document is usually previewed, printed, and closed without saving. However, you can certainly save the merged document if you wish to save a record of it. If a merged document contains errors, you can close it without saving, edit the main document or data source, and then conduct the merge again.

DEVELOP YOUR SKILLS 7.7.1
Conduct the Merge

In this exercise, you will use the Preview Results group on the Mailings tab to review your letters before you perform the merge. Then you will complete the merge on the screen.

1. Choose **Mailings→Preview Results→Preview Results** from the Ribbon to view the data from the first record.

2. Use the **navigation buttons** in the Preview Results group to scroll through all your merged documents.

3. Choose **Mailings→Finish→Finish & Merge** from the Ribbon.

4. Choose **Edit Individual Documents** from the menu to merge the letters on the screen.

5. Click **OK** to merge all records.

6. **Scroll** through the letters and scan their contents.
   Notice that there is one letter for each record in the data source.

7. **Close** the merged document without saving.

8. Choose **Mailings→Preview Results→Preview Results** again to display the main document instead of the preview.

9. Leave the main document **open** for the next exercise.

7.8 Working with Merge Problems

Video Lesson labyrinthelab.com/videos

Several common errors can cause a merge to produce incorrect results. The merged document (or preview) will usually provide clues as to why a merge fails to produce the intended results. Once you identify an error in the merged document, such as leaving out a comma or space before or after a merge field, you can make changes to the main document or the data source. You can then conduct the merge again to determine if the error was fixed. Repeat this process until the merge works as intended.

Common Merge Problems

Several problems are common in merges. These problems and their solutions are described in the following Quick Reference table.

QUICK REFERENCE	DEALING WITH COMMON MERGE PROBLEMS
Problem	**Solution**
The exact same error appears in every merge letter.	The problem is in the main document, since it occurs in every merge letter. Correct the error in the main document and perform the merge again.
Some letters in the merged document are missing data.	This occurs because some records in the data source are missing data. Add data to the necessary fields in the data source, or modify the main document or merged letters to account for the missing data.
Some letters in the merged document have incorrect data.	The problem is in the data source, since it does not affect every letter in the merged document. Correct the data errors in the data source and perform the merge again.

DEVELOP YOUR SKILLS 7.8.1
Fix Merge Problems

In this exercise, you will examine your document for merge problems. Refer to the previous table if you need help solving them. The following steps are a guide to assist you. They do not address all the possible problems that you may encounter; they do, however, address one specific error that was made intentionally. You will insert a comma after the First Name field.

1. Position the **insertion point** after the <<First Name>> merge field, and then **type** a comma.

2. Conduct the **Finish & Merge** process again to review and fix problems in the merged document.

3. Browse through the entire document, from beginning to end, and look for any errors. Note errors in a separate Word document or on a piece of paper. Indicate how often the errors occur (in every merged letter or just one).

4. If you find an error that occurs in *every merged letter,* such as the one you corrected with the missing comma, **close** the merged document without saving and **edit** the main document, and then **save** it.

5. If you find a data error in *just one letter,* such as the missing *Facilities* department name for Mr. Adams, close the merged document without saving it.

- Choose **Mailings→Start Mail Merge→Edit Recipient List**  from the Ribbon.

- When the Mail Merge Recipients dialog box appears, highlight the **Data Source** in the bottom-left corner of the dialog box, and click the **Edit** button.

- After you fix any errors, click **OK**, and then click **Yes** when the message appears asking if you want to update the data.

- Click **OK** to close the Mail Merge Recipients dialog box.

6. When you have corrected any errors, execute the **merge** again.

7. **Close** the merged document without saving it.

8. **Save** 🖫 and **close** Policy Manual Letter Main.

7.9 Using Envelopes and Labels with Mail Merge

Video Lesson   labyrinthelab.com/videos

When you choose Mailings→Start Mail Merge→Start Mail Merge 📄 from the Ribbon, Word presents you with options for the type of main document you want to create. In addition to form letters, you can use envelopes, labels, and other types of documents as main documents. The merged document's title bar reflects the type of merge performed. For example, when you conduct the merge for envelopes the first time, the name of the merged document is Envelopes1; you may change the name and save it if you wish.

You can use the same data source for various main documents. For example, you can use the same data source for envelopes and mailing labels that you used for the form letter.

Generating Envelopes with Mail Merge

You can use Mail Merge to generate an envelope for each record in a data source. Mail Merge lets you choose the envelope size and formats. The standard business (Size 10) envelope is the default. You will check your printer to see how to place the envelopes in it for printing. For example, you may need to know which side should be facing up and which way the flap is facing.

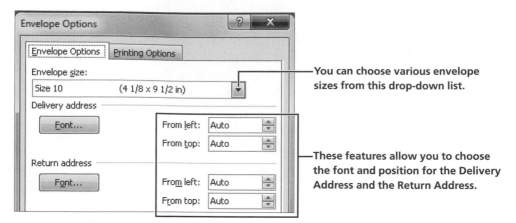

You can choose various envelope sizes from this drop-down list.

These features allow you to choose the font and position for the Delivery Address and the Return Address.

 If you are using envelopes with the company name and address preprinted, then you will not use any Return Address options here.

DEVELOP YOUR SKILLS 7.9.1

Choose an Envelope Size and Attach a Data Source

In this exercise, you will choose an envelope as the main document and connect the Policy Manual Letter Data file to the envelope.

1. Start a **new** blank document.

2. Choose **Mailings→Start Mail Merge→Start Mail Merge**  from the Ribbon, and then choose **Envelopes** from the menu.

3. When the Envelope Options dialog box appears, if necessary, choose **Size 10** from the Envelope Size list.
   This is the standard envelope size for business correspondence.

4. Click **OK** to apply the settings to the document.
   The envelope main document appears in the Word window although right now, it doesn't look any different. You will set up the envelope main document in a moment, and you will see the envelope layout on the screen.

Connect the Data Source

5. Choose **Mailings→Start Mail Merge→Select Recipients** [icon] from the Ribbon, and then choose **Use Existing List** from the menu.

6. When the Select Data Source dialog box appears, navigate to your file storage location and **open** Policy Manual Letter Data from the Lesson 07 folder.

7. Stay in the **Mailings** tab for the next topic.

Arranging the Envelope

Video Lesson labyrinthelab.com/videos

You can insert an address block in the envelope main document. An envelope main document can be saved like any other main document, allowing you to use it over and over to generate envelopes from a data source. The following illustration shows the envelope main document that you will set up in the next exercise.

─The return address is typed in the top-left corner of the envelope main document.
Remember, if you have preprinted business envelopes, skip this step.

The envelope has a rectangular placeholder for the address block. You must click the placeholder before inserting the address block.

Green·Clean¶
719·Coronado· Drive¶
San·Diego,·CA·92103¶
⚓   ¶

Mr.·D'Andre·Adams¶
3344·Culver·Drive¶
San·Diego,·CA·92102¶

DEVELOP YOUR SKILLS 7.9.2

Merge to Envelopes

In this exercise, you will position the return address and the address block on the envelope, and then you will merge the envelope main document with the data source.

Set Up the Envelope

1. If necessary, turn on the **formatting marks**, and then **type** the return address, starting at the first paragraph symbol in the upper-left corner of the envelope, as shown here.

2. Position the **insertion point** next to the paragraph symbol toward the center bottom half of the envelope to display the address block placeholder.

Green· Clean¶
719·Coronado· Drive¶
San· Diego,·CA·92103¶¶
¶

3. Choose **Mailings→Write & Insert Fields→Address Block** [icon] from the Ribbon.

4. Click **OK** to accept the default address block settings.
   This is the same Insert Address Block dialog box you used to insert the address block in the form letter. An Address Block field is inserted in the placeholder box. Word will merge the address information from the data source into this location when the merge is conducted.

Preview the Merge

5. Choose **Mailings→Preview Results→Preview Results** [icon] from the Ribbon to display the first record from the data source in the envelope.

6. Use the **navigation buttons** in the Preview Results group to scroll through all your merged envelopes.

7. Choose **Mailings→Finish→Finish & Merge** [icon] from the Ribbon.

8. Choose **Edit Individual Documents** from the menu, and then click **OK** to merge all the records.

9. Turn **off** the formatting marks from the Ribbon.

10. **Scroll** through the envelopes, and notice that there is one envelope for each record in the data source.
    You could use the envelopes for mailing the letters created in the previous exercises, because they are generated from the same data source.

11. If necessary, fix any problems with the mail merge.

12. When you finish, **save** [icon] the merged document as `Policy Manual Envelopes` in the Lesson 07 folder, and then **close** it.

13. Turn **off** the Preview Results button, and then **save** the envelope in the Lesson 07 folder as `Policy Manual Envelope Main` and **close** it.

Generating Labels with Mail Merge

Video Lesson labyrinthelab.com/videos

You can use Mail Merge to generate mailing labels for each record in a data source. Mail Merge lets you choose the label format, sheet size, and other specifications. It also lets you insert an address block and other fields in the main document. Like other main documents, a labels main document, as well as the merged document, can be saved for future use. The following illustration shows a portion of the labels main document that you will set up in the next exercise.

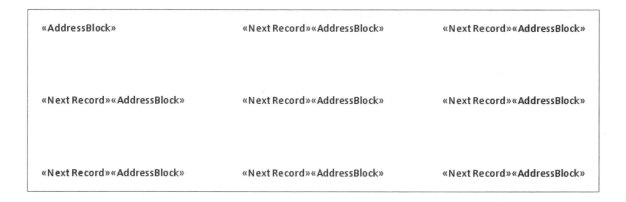

«AddressBlock» «Next Record»«AddressBlock» «Next Record»«AddressBlock»

«Next Record»«AddressBlock» «Next Record»«AddressBlock» «Next Record»«AddressBlock»

«Next Record»«AddressBlock» «Next Record»«AddressBlock» «Next Record»«AddressBlock»

Using Label Options

The Label Options dialog box allows you to choose printer options and the type of label you will use for your merge. You will find a number on the package of labels you purchase that may correspond to the Product Number in the Label Options dialog box. If you buy a brand name not included in the Label Vendors list, you can match your label size with the label size in the Label Information section.

Choose the appropriate printer information in this area.

Choose the product brand from this drop-down list.

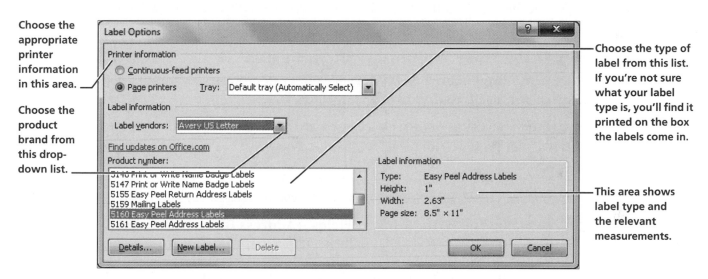

Choose the type of label from this list. If you're not sure what your label type is, you'll find it printed on the box the labels come in.

This area shows label type and the relevant measurements.

Use Mail Merge to Generate Mailing Labels

In this exercise, you will set up a labels main document, and then you will merge the labels main document with the data source used in the previous exercises.

1. Start a **new** blank document.

2. If necessary, choose **Home→Paragraph→Show/Hide** ¶ from the Ribbon to display formatting marks.

3. Choose **Mailings→Start Mail Merge→Start Mail Merge** 📄 from the Ribbon, and then choose **Labels** from the menu.

4. Follow these steps to choose a label:

A Scroll through the options and choose **Avery US Letter** from the Label Vendors drop-down list.

B Scroll through the list options and then choose **5160 Easy Peel Address Labels** from the Product Number list.

C Click **OK**.

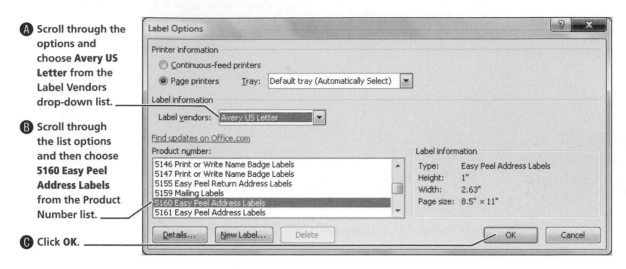

The labels main document appears in the Word window.

Labels are contained in a Word table, but don't worry. You don't have to be a table expert to create labels. By default, table grid lines don't appear when you create labels.

Connect the Data Source

5. Choose **Mailings→Start Mail Merge→Select Recipients** from the Ribbon, and then choose **Use Existing List** from the menu.

6. When the Select Data Source dialog box opens, navigate to your file storage location and **open** Policy Manual Letter Data. Make sure the insertion point is in the first address label position.
Notice that the space for the first label is blank and all the rest have a <<Next Record>> code in them. You will add the Address Block merge fields with the next few steps.

7. Choose **Mailings→Write & Insert Fields→Address Block** from the Ribbon.

8. Click **OK** to insert the address block code in the first label.

9. Choose **Mailings→Write & Insert Fields→Update Labels** from the Ribbon to place the address block in all of the labels.
Your addresses will fit the labels better if you remove Word's additional spacing.

10. Press Ctrl + A to select the entire document.

11. Choose **Home→Styles** from the Ribbon.

12. Choose the **No Spacing** style from the Quick Styles gallery.

13. Choose **Mailings→Preview Results→Preview Results** from the Ribbon to see how the labels will look when you print them, and then turn off the Preview Results command.

Conduct the Merge

14. Choose **Mailings→Finish→Finish & Merge** [icon] from the Ribbon.

15. Choose **Edit Individual Documents** from the menu.

16. When the Merge to New Document dialog box appears, click **OK** to merge all the records.

17. **Close** your merged document without saving it.

18. **Save** [icon] the labels main document in the Lesson 07 folder as `Merge Labels`, and then **close** it.

7.10 Concepts Review

Concepts Review   labyrinthelab.com/word10

To check your knowledge of the key concepts introduced in this lesson, complete the Concepts Review quiz by going to the URL listed above. If your classroom is using Labyrinth eLab, you may complete the Concepts Review quiz from within your eLab course.

Reinforce Your Skills

Apply Quick Styles to a Document

In this exercise, you will apply Quick Styles to a document. Then you will copy a style using the Format Painter, and finally you will change the Theme color to alter the look of the style.

Change the Quick Styles Style Set

1. **Open** rs-Instructor Profiles from the Lesson 07 folder.

2. **Select** in the heading at the top of the document.

3. Choose **Home→Styles→Change Styles** 🅰 from the Ribbon.

4. Choose **Fancy** from the Style Set submenu.

Apply a Style

5. Click the **More** ▾ button on the Quick Styles gallery to display the entire gallery.

6. Choose the **Title** style to format the document heading.

7. Position the **insertion point** in the heading *Tanya Walton* below the main heading.

8. Choose **Heading 2** from the Quick Styles gallery. Keep the insertion point in the heading *Tanya Walton*.

Copy the Quick Style

9. Choose **Home→Clipboard** from the Ribbon.

10. Use the **Format Painter** 🖌 to copy the Heading 2 style to the other instructor headings. *Remember, double-clicking the Format Painter keeps the feature turned on until you turn it off.*

11. Turn off the Format Painter.

Change the Theme Color

You may recall that the look of Quick Styles is based on the current document theme.

12. Choose **Page Layout→Theme**s**→Theme Colors** ◼ from the Ribbon.

13. Choose **Urban** from the list.

14. **Save** 💾 the file, and **close** it.

Create, Modify, and Delete a Character Style

In this exercise, you will create a character Quick Style. You will create the style by formatting text with the formats you want in your style. Then you will modify your new style, and finally you will delete it.

1. **Open** rs-Recycle Computers from the Lesson 07 folder.

2. **Select** *Wellsville Donation Center* in the table *Where To Take Your Computer Equipment*.

Format the Text

3. Choose **Home→Font→Font Color** [A] menu ▼ from the Ribbon.

4. Choose the color in **column 6, row 5**: Red, Accent 2, Darker 25%.

5. Choose **Home→Font→Bold** [B] from the Ribbon.

6. Choose **Home→Font→Font Size** [11 ▼] menu ▼ from the Ribbon, and choose **16 pt**.

Create the Style

7. Keep the text selected, and if necessary, click the **dialog box launcher** [◲] in the bottom-right corner of the Styles group on the Home tab.
   This opens the Styles task pane.

8. Click the **New Style** [⅍] button in the bottom-left corner of the Styles task pane.
   Notice that the Formatting area of the dialog box has taken on the formatting from the selected text in the document, so the only thing remaining is to give the style a name.

9. Type **My Character Style** in the Name area at the top of the dialog box.

10. Choose **Character** from the Style Type drop-down list and click **OK**.

Apply the Style

11. Use the **Quick Styles** gallery to apply the new character style to *Woodridge Donation Center* in the table.

12. Use the **Styles** task pane to apply **My Character Style** to *Elk Grove Donation Center* in the table.

13. **Apply** your new style to the remaining donation center names, using either the Quick Styles gallery or the Styles task pane.

Modify the Style

You've decided that the point size in your style is too large, so you will change the point size, and all of the text formatted with that style will update with the change.

14. Hover the **mouse pointer** over My Character Style in the Styles task pane and click the drop-down arrow, and then choose **Modify**.

15. Choose **14 pt** from the Font Size drop-down menu, and then click **OK**.
    Notice that all donation center names reformatted to 14 pt.

Delete the Style

16. Hover the **mouse pointer** over My Character Style in the Styles task pane to display the drop-down arrow.

17. Click the **arrow**, and choose **Delete My Character Style** from the menu.

18. When the message appears confirming the deletion, click **Yes**.
    Notice that Word removed the style from the names of the donation centers and deleted the style from the Quick Styles gallery and the Styles task pane.

19. Click the **Close** ☒ button in the upper-right corner of the Styles task pane to close it.

20. **Save** 🖫 the file, and **close** it.

REINFORCE YOUR SKILLS 7.3
Set Up a New Mail Merge

In this exercise, you will set up a main document and a data source. You will remove unnecessary fields from the data source, sort the data, and execute the merge.

Set Up the Data Source

1. **Open** the rs-Fundraiser Main document from the Lesson 07 folder.

2. Choose **Mailings→Start Mail Merge→Start Mail Merge** 📄 from the Ribbon, and then choose **Letters** from the menu.

3. Choose **Mailings→Start Mail Merge→Select Recipients** 📇 from the Ribbon, and then choose **Type New List** from the menu.

4. Click the **Customize Columns** button in the New Address List dialog box to display the Customize Address List dialog box.

5. Use the **Delete** button in the dialog box to remove the following fields (You must select the field names on the list before clicking Delete.):
   - Address Line 2
   - Country or Region
   - Home Phone
   - E-mail Address

6. Click **OK** to complete the changes to the data source.

Enter Data

7. **Enter** the following data into your new data source:

Mr. Sean Corn 308 Alhambra Avenue Monterey Park, CA 91754 626-555-9876	Mr. Craig Dostie Whole Life, Inc. 31200 Erwin Street Woodland Hills, CA 91367 818-555-1711	Ms. Alexia Lopez 2134 Harbor Blvd. Costa Mesa, CA 92626 714-555-9855
Ms. Winston Boey Pasadena City College Pasadena, CA 91104 626-555-1234	Ms. Phyllis Coen Pasadena City College 4745 Buffin Avenue Fremont, CA 94536 408-555-4950	Ms. Margaret Wong Popcorn Video 1308 West Ramona Blvd. Alhambra, CA 91803 818-555-8883

8. Click **OK** when you finish entering the data.

9. Use the **Save Address List** box to navigate to your exercise files.

10. **Save** the data source in the Lesson 07 folder as `rs-Address Data`.

Sort the List

11. Choose **Mailings→Start Mail Merge→Edit Recipient List** from the Ribbon.

12. Click the **Last Name** column heading to sort the records on the Last Name field, as shown here.

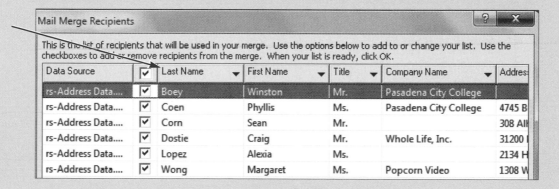

13. Click **OK** to return to the main document.

Set Up the Form Letter

14. Use the following guidelines to insert codes as shown in the following main document:

- Replace **Today's Date** with a date code that will update automatically.
- Insert the **Address Block** merge field below the date (as shown in the following illustration), using the first and last name only format.
- Insert an **appropriate greeting** line followed by a colon.
- Insert the **Work_Phone** merge field as shown in the last paragraph.

West Coast Youth Services
2500 Ocean Avenue
Monterey Park, CA 91753
310-555-6459

Today's Date

«AddressBlock»

«GreetingLine»

We have decided to hold the annual fundraiser on July 15 in Los Angeles. As you know, last year's fundraiser was a huge success. We hope to make this year's fundraiser equally successful. This will require early planning and effective advertising.

Please RSVP as soon as possible. I must know if you can participate in the event. I would truly appreciate your support and commitment.

Also, I have your updated address. But I may need an updated telephone number. I currently have your telephone number listed as «Work_Phone». Please contact me and let me know if your number has changed.

Sincerely,

Cynthia Thompson
Fundraising Director

Conduct the Merge

15. **Preview** your letters and **correct** any errors you find in the main document or data source.

16. Now **complete** the merge, using the **Edit Individual Documents** option.

17. When you finish, **close** the merged document without saving it.

18. Turn off Preview Results, and then **save and close** the document.

REINFORCE YOUR SKILLS 7.4

Generate Mailing Labels

In this exercise, you will create a labels main document. You will merge the labels document with rs-Address Data.

1. Start a **new** Word document.

2. Choose **Mailings→Start Mail Merge→Start Mail Merge** 🗋 from the Ribbon.

3. Choose **Labels** from the menu.

4. If necessary, choose **5160** from the Product Number box.

5. Click **OK** to apply the settings to the document.

Attach the Data Source

6. Choose **Mailings→Start Mail Merge→Select Recipients** 🗐 from the Ribbon.

7. Click **Use Existing List** from the menu.

8. Choose rs-Address Data from the Lesson 07 folder.

Arrange the Labels

9. Choose **Mailings→Write & Insert Fields→Address Block** 🗐 from the Ribbon.

10. Click **OK** to insert the address block code in the first label.

11. Choose **Mailings→Write & Insert Fields→Update Labels** 🗐 from the Ribbon.
    This populates the sheet with codes, ensuring that labels can be positioned at all locations on the sheet.

12. **Press** [Ctrl]+[A] to select the entire document.

13. Choose **Home→Styles** from the Ribbon.

14. Choose the **No Spacing** style from the Quick Styles gallery to remove Word's extra spacing.

Merge the Main Document and Data Source

15. Choose **Mailings→Preview Results→Preview Results** 🔍 from the Ribbon.

16. **Preview** your labels, and then **complete** the merge using the **Edit Individual Documents** option from the menu.

17. Click **OK** to merge all records.

18. Observe your labels. You should see one label for each record.

19. When you finish, **close** the merged document without saving it.

20. Turn off Preview Results, and then **save and close** the file.

Apply Your Skills

APPLY YOUR SKILLS 7.1

Work with Views

In this exercise, you will use the Split command to view a document, and then you will open a second document and use the View Side by Side view to compare the documents.

Split a Document Window

1. **Open** the as-TrainRight Qualifications document from the Lesson 07 folder.

2. **Split** the Word window horizontally, with the split bar approximately in the middle of the screen.
   - Ask your instructor to initial that this has been done successfully. _____

3. **Remove the split** from the Word window.
   - Ask your instructor to initial that this has been done successfully. _____

Use the Arrange All View

4. Position the **insertion point** at the top of the document.

5. **Open** the as-Qualifications document from the Lesson 07 folder.

6. Use the View Side by Side command, and **scroll** through each window separately to compare the formatted and unformatted documents.

7. **View** the two open documents side by side.

8. **Scroll** through the document at the same time.

9. **Close** both files, and then **maximize** the Word window.

Merge a Form Letter with a Data Source

In this exercise, you will create a new main document letter. Then you will create a new address list, but you will remove any unnecessary fields first. Finally, you will execute the merge.

1. Use the **Mailings** tab and the following guidelines to set up a form letter and data source:
   - Use the as-Health Club Main document from the Lesson 07 folder.
   - Your data source should contain only the **three records** shown after the letter below. Remove any **unused fields** from the data source.
   - **Save** the data source document as **as-Health Club Data** in the Lesson 07 folder.
   - Insert the **date** in the form letter as a field that updates automatically.
   - Insert an **address block** and **greeting** of your choice.
   - Insert the **work phone number** field in the appropriate location.

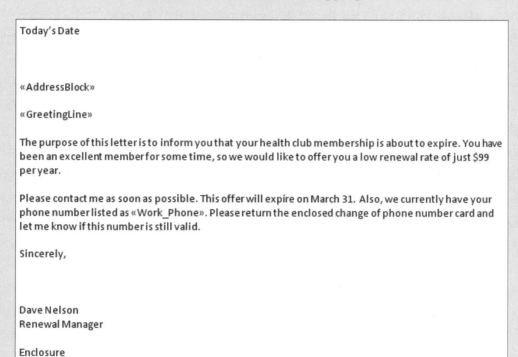

Today's Date

«AddressBlock»

«GreetingLine»

The purpose of this letter is to inform you that your health club membership is about to expire. You have been an excellent member for some time, so we would like to offer you a low renewal rate of just $99 per year.

Please contact me as soon as possible. This offer will expire on March 31. Also, we currently have your phone number listed as «Work_Phone». Please return the enclosed change of phone number card and let me know if this number is still valid.

Sincerely,

Dave Nelson
Renewal Manager

Enclosure

Mr. David Roth	Mrs. Tammy Simpson	Mr. Jason Williams
760 Maple Avenue	Barkers Books	2233 Crystal Street
Fremont, CA 94538	312 Tennessee Street	San Mateo, CA 94403
510-555-9090	Richmond, VA 94804	415-555-2312
	510-555-2233	

2. **Merge** the form letter with the data source.

3. Turn off **Preview Results, save** the document, and then **close** it.

4. If necessary, **save** any changes to your main document, and then **close** it.

Generate Envelopes

In this exercise, you will create a new main envelope document and execute the merge.

1. Use the **Mailings** tab on the Ribbon and these guidelines to set up an envelope main document:
   - Use a **standard size 10** envelope.
   - Use as-Health Club Data as the **data source**.
   - Use the **return address** of your choice.
   - Position the **insertion point** in the placeholder toward the center bottom half of the envelope and insert the **default address block**.

2. **Save** the envelope main document in your Lesson 07 folder as **as-Health Club Envelope**.

3. **Merge** the envelope main document with the data source.

4. **Close** the merged document without saving it.

5. If necessary, **save** any changes to the envelope main document, and then **close** it.

Critical Thinking & Work-Readiness Skills

In the course of working through the following Microsoft Office-based Critical Thinking exercises, you will also be utilizing various work-readiness skills, some of which are listed next to each exercise. Go to labyrinthelab.com/ workreadiness to learn more about the work-readiness skills.

7.1 Style an Employee Policy Manual

Jenna is formatting the new employee policy manual. Open ct-Employee Manual Draft from your Lesson 7 folder and, using Style tools, give it a consistent and professional look. Format the company logo as necessary. Number all of the topics. Ask yourself: Are there any missing that I might reasonably want to see covered in an employee manual? Add a note to the end of the file suggesting topics you would like to see covered. Save the file as **ct-Employee Manual Draft 2**.

WORK-READINESS SKILLS APPLIED
- Showing responsibility
- Reading
- Evaluating information

7.2 Move Sections

Jenna wants to reorganize the manual so that the information flows in a more logical way. If necessary, open ct-Employee Manual Draft 2 and save it to your Lesson 7 folder as **ct-Employee Manual Draft 3**. Use the Navigation pane to move the president's Welcome message to before Company History and move the Company Mission to before the Company Vision. Rearrange the other sections as you see fit. Use the Split Bar to keep the top portion of the manual visible as you scroll through the document in the bottom pane looking for other thing to improve. Make any changes you feel are necessary and then save and close the file. If working in a group, discuss why you decided to organize the manual as you did. If working alone, type your answer in a Word document named **ct-Questions** saved to your Lesson 7 folder.

WORK-READINESS SKILLS APPLIED
- Reading
- Evaluating information
- Organizing information

7.3 Use Mail Merge

Jenna decides to ask for help from some outside consultants who are experts in employee policy documentation. Create a mail merge data source from the ct-Consultants file in your Lesson 7 folder and save it as **ct-Consultant Data Source**. Next, create a form letter thanking the consultants for help and asking them to send you feedback at their earliest convenience. Insert the appropriate address block and greeting line, using the data source, and save the form letter to your Lesson 7 folder as **ct-Dear Consultants Merged**.

WORK-READINESS SKILLS APPLIED
- Exercising leadership
- Using computers to process information
- Writing

Creating a Research Paper

LEARNING OBJECTIVES

After studying this lesson, you will be able to:

- Insert footnotes and endnotes in a research paper
- Add headers and footers to documents
- Place captions on figures
- Generate a table of figures
- Create templates

In this lesson, you will learn about research papers, a requirement for nearly every undergraduate and graduate student, and for many professionally employed individuals. You will use Word to develop a research paper using widely accepted style conventions. Your paper will include footnotes, endnotes, a header, and a table of figures. Then you will create a research paper template to simplify writing future research papers.

Researching Internet Commerce

Brian Simpson works as a customer service representative at Green Clean while continuing his undergraduate work in marketing at a small private college. Brian was assigned the task of writing a research paper. The main topic must be on Internet commerce, and since Brian is also interested in the environment, he puts his own spin on the paper to include what effect e-commerce has had on the environment.

Brian uses Word 2010 to set up the research paper. Following the Modern Language Association's (MLA) handbook, he uses a header, footnotes, and a table of figures in his paper. Brian finds that the Footnote feature makes it easy to insert information about research sources into his paper.

green clean

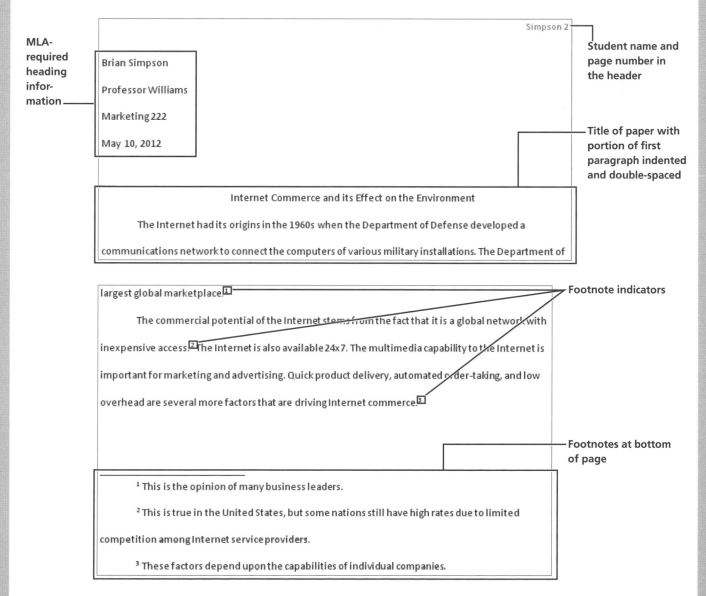

MLA-required heading information

Brian Simpson

Professor Williams

Marketing 222

May 10, 2012

Simpson 2

Student name and page number in the header

Title of paper with portion of first paragraph indented and double-spaced

Internet Commerce and its Effect on the Environment

The Internet had its origins in the 1960s when the Department of Defense developed a communications network to connect the computers of various military installations. The Department of

largest global marketplace.[1]

The commercial potential of the Internet stems from the fact that it is a global network with inexpensive access.[2] The Internet is also available 24x7. The multimedia capability to the Internet is important for marketing and advertising. Quick product delivery, automated order-taking, and low overhead are several more factors that are driving Internet commerce.[3]

Footnote indicators

Footnotes at bottom of page

[1] This is the opinion of many business leaders.

[2] This is true in the United States, but some nations still have high rates due to limited competition among Internet service providers.

[3] These factors depend upon the capabilities of individual companies.

8.1 Using Research Paper Styles

There are several documentation styles, each with their own specific formatting requirements. The MLA style has been the standard for undergraduate and graduate research papers for many years.

Understanding the MLA Documentation Style

Video Lesson labyrinthelab.com/videos

The MLA publishes the *Modern Language Association Handbook for Writers of Research Papers*. The MLA style has very specific formatting requirements, some of which are already defaults within Microsoft Word. For example, all four of Word's default margins are one inch, which complies with the MLA margin requirement. You can visit the MLA website at www.mla.org for detailed information. Following is an overview of the MLA style guidelines:

■ MLA style requires a header with the student's name followed by the page number aligned on the right one-half inch from the top of every page.

■ The student name, professor, course, and date lines are positioned at the top-left of the first page and are double-spaced. Note that MLA does not require a separate title page for the research paper.

■ The title of the paper follows the date line and extra line.

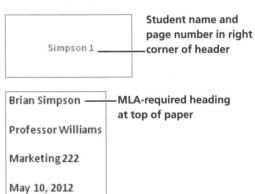

An extra line between the date and paper title

May·10,·2012¶

¶

Internet·Commerce·and·its·Effect·on·the·Environment¶

■ The first line of each paragraph is indented one-half inch, and the line spacing requirement is double-space with the extra spacing removed after the paragraph.

Paragraph indented and double-spaced

The Internet had its origins in the 1960s when the Department of Defense developed a communications network to connect the computers of various military installations. The Department of Defense removed its computers from this network in the 1980s and turned over the control to the

■ A superscript number appears at the end of the text to indicate a footnote or endnote. The actual footnote or endnote text uses the same formatting as the rest of the document.

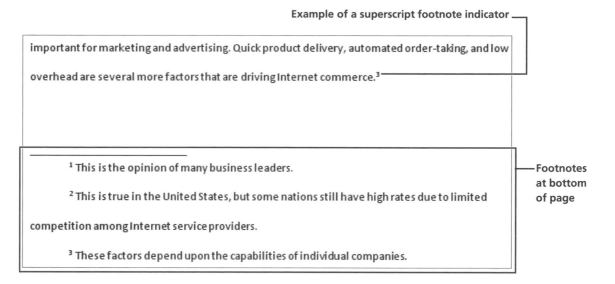

Example of a superscript footnote indicator

important for marketing and advertising. Quick product delivery, automated order-taking, and low

overhead are several more factors that are driving Internet commerce.[3]

¹ This is the opinion of many business leaders.

² This is true in the United States, but some nations still have high rates due to limited

competition among Internet service providers.

³ These factors depend upon the capabilities of individual companies.

Footnotes at bottom of page

■ A citation appears in parentheses at the end of the line you are referencing, instead of a superscripted footnote or endnote indicator. The citation usually contains the author's last name and possibly a page number if referencing a page in a book.

Example of a citation

The environmental outlook is indeed bright: according to the latest study by Carnegie Mellon

University, more than half (about 65%) of total emissions was produced by consumers driving to and

from retail stores as opposed to buying online (Swaney).

■ A separate Works Cited page is added to the end of the research paper, listing, in alphabetical order, all citations referenced in the document.

Example of a Works Cited page

Works Cited

Fowler, Geoffrey. The Green Side of Online Shopping. 3 March 2009. 14 March 2012

<http://blogs.wsj.com/digits/2009/03/03/the-green-side-of-online-shopping/tab/article/>.

Swaney, Chriss. Carnegie Mellon Study Finds Shopping Online Results in Less Environmental Impact. 3 March 2009.

10 March 2012 <http://www.cit.cmu.edu/media/press/2009/03_03_online_shopping.html>.

8.2 Working with Footnotes, Endnotes, and Citations

Video Lesson labyrinthelab.com/videos

Footnotes, endnotes, and citations are important parts of most research papers. You use them to comment on or cite a reference to a designated part of the text. Footnotes appear at the bottoms of pages; endnotes, as the name implies, appear at the end of a document or section; and citations appear on a separate Works Cited page at the end of the document. The Works Cited page is another name for a bibliography.

For the sake of simplicity, the following topics use the term *footnote* only. All details described for footnotes apply equally to endnotes.

Inserting Footnotes

The References tab of the Ribbon contains many of the commands you will use for this research paper project. You can insert footnotes using the buttons in the Footnotes group, keyboard shortcuts, and the Footnote and Endnote dialog box. Word automatically numbers each footnote and renumbers them if you add or remove one.

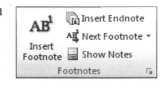

FROM THE KEYBOARD

Alt + Ctrl + F to insert a footnote

When you insert a footnote, Word automatically inserts a superscripted number for it in your text at the location of the insertion point.

marketplace.[1]

Using the Footnote and Endnote Dialog Box

This dialog box offers another method for inserting notes, but additionally it provides options for controlling the position, format, and other aspects of notes. You can even create custom footnote marks.

This is where you can choose to insert either a footnote or an endnote.

You can choose from several formats for footnote and endnote reference marks. You can also type a custom mark or choose a custom character from the Symbol dialog box.

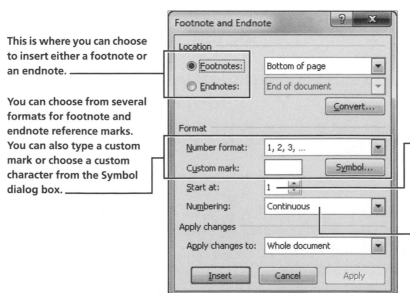

The Start At option is useful if you have a large project organized into multiple documents. In this situation, you can specify a starting number for the footnotes and endnotes in each document.

Here you specify whether numbering should be continuous throughout the document or restart at each new section or page.

Inserting Footnote Links

When you insert a footnote, Word inserts a footnote reference mark in the document, and the mark is linked to a corresponding footnote. The following illustration shows a footnote reference mark and the corresponding footnote at the bottom of the page.

This is the footnote reference mark in the main portion of the document. It matches the number or symbol in the footnote.

The footnote text is typed at the bottom of the page. Word adds a note separator line above the footnotes and inserts the appropriate numbers.

overhead are several more factors that are driving Internet commerce[3]

Internet commerce will be a driving force in the global economy of the twenty-first century.

There are still obstacles to overcome, but technology and market forces will propel this new commercial

medium forward at a rapid pace.

---

[1] This is the opinion of many business leaders.
[2] This is true in the United States, but some nations still have high rates due to limited competition among Internet service providers.
[3] These factors depend upon the capabilities of individual companies.

Using Citations

A citation is used to refer to material you obtained from an outside source that you are using in the paper. The source information can be entered when you insert the citation, or you can insert a placeholder and edit the source data later. The citation appears inside parentheses at the end of the cited material; this notation takes the place of the superscript number that is placed for a footnote or endnote.

This option opens the Create Source dialog box, where you enter the source's data at the same time you insert the citation.

This option lets you insert a placeholder for the citation and then go back later to update the source information.

Inserting a Citation

The Insert Citation command is found in the Citations & Bibliography group on the References tab of the Ribbon. Immediately following the text and before the ending punctuation, a note (sometimes referred to as a p-note because it appears inside parentheses) is placed citing the author's last name, if available, or the document title. Before inserting the citation, it's a good idea to choose the style of documentation you are using, for example, MLA, APA, or Chicago. You will learn more about this later in this lesson.

In addition to the MLA documentation style, two other popular styles are American Psychological Association (APA) and The Chicago Manual of Style (CMS).

A truck delivering numerous packages along its way is the largest environmental savings,

as it uses less energy per package than if the consumers had driven to the shops

themselves (Fowler).

This is an example of a citation, where the author's last name is placed inside parentheses at the end of a paragraph. Notice the citation is after the text but before the period. A common mistake is to place the citation after the period.

DEVELOP YOUR SKILLS 8.2.1
Insert Footnotes and Citations

In this exercise, you will create a research paper and insert footnotes and citations in it. You will also look at the footnotes in different views.

1. **Open** the Internet Research document from the Lesson 08 folder.
   Feel free to turn the formatting marks on or off as needed during this lesson.

2. If necessary, switch to **Print Layout** 🔲 view.
   Footnotes may differ in appearance depending on the view you are using, as you will see later.

3. Position the **insertion point** at the top of the document and **type** the four lines of text above the title, **tapping** [Enter] once after each line, including the last line:

Brian·Simpson¶

Professor·Williams¶

Marketing·222¶

May·10,·2012¶

¶

               Internet·Commerce·and·Its·Effect·on·the·Environment¶

    The·Internet·had·its·origins·in·the·1960s·when·the·Department·of·Defense·developed·a·communications·network·to·connect·the·computers·of·various·military·installations.·The·Department·of·Defense·removed·its·computers·from·this·network·in·the·1980s·and·turned·over·the·control·to·the·National·Science·Foundation·(NSF).·In·1992,·the·U.S.·government·withdrew·funding·from·the·NSF·and·encouraged·private·companies·to·administer·and·control·the·"Internet."·It·was·at·this·point·that·Internet·commerce·was·born.·Companies·both·large·and·small·suddenly·realized·the·enormous·marketing·potential·of·this·global·computer·network.·In·fact,·by·2007,·the·Internet·has·no·doubt·become·the·largest·global·marketplace.¶

    The·commercial·potential·of·the·Internet·stems·from·the·fact·that·it·is·a·global·network·with·

The additional line space between the date and the title is an MLA requirement. Notice also that the paragraph text is double-spaced and the extra space after the paragraphs has been removed, per MLA requirements.

Insert a Footnote

4. Position the **insertion point** to the right of the period at the end of the first paragraph.

5. Choose **References→Footnotes→Insert Footnote** ⟨AB¹⟩ from the Ribbon.

6. Follow these steps to complete the footnote:

Ⓐ The footnote area appears at the bottom of the page. Word automatically inserts both a separator line and the correct superscript number.

¹ This is the opinion of many business leaders.

Ⓑ **Type** the text shown in the footnote area.

7. Position the **insertion point** in the appropriate places, then use **References→Footnotes→Insert Footnote** from the Ribbon to insert the remaining two footnotes shown in the following illustration.

The commercial potential of the Internet stems from the fact that it is a global network with inexpensive access.² The Internet is also available 24x7. The multimedia capability to the Internet is important for marketing and advertising. Quick product delivery, automated order-taking, and low overhead are several more factors that are driving Internet commerce.³

Internet commerce will be a driving force in the global economy of the twenty-first century. There are still obstacles to overcome, but technology and market forces will propel this new commercial medium forward at a rapid pace.

¹ This is the opinion of many business leaders.
² This is true in the United States, but some nations still have high rates due to limited competition among Internet service providers.
³ These factors depend upon the capabilities of individual companies.

Notice that the formatting of the footnotes does not adhere to MLA requirements. You will fix this a little later in this lesson.

8. **Type** the following paragraphs after the paragraph beginning *Internet Commerce will be*...

> The environmental outlook is indeed bright: according to the latest study by Carnegie Mellon University, more than half (about 65%) of total emissions was produced by consumers driving to and from retail stores as opposed to buying online.
>
> Geoffrey Fowler, in his March 3, 2009 article on the Wall Street Journal website, cited the following environmental benefits to e-commerce shopping:
>
> - Uses about one-third less energy than conventional retail shopping
> - Uses a one-third smaller carbon footprint than a standard building
> - A truck delivering numerous packages along its way is the largest environmental savings, as it uses less energy per package than if the consumers had driven to the shops themselves.

Change the Style to MLA

9. Choose **References→Citations & Bibliography→MLA Sixth Edition** from the Ribbon.

Insert a Citation as a New Source

10. Position the **insertion point** between the word *online* and the period at the end of the first paragraph on page 2 and **tap** the [Spacebar].

> The environmental outlook is indeed br
>
> University, more than half (about 65%) of total e
>
> from retail stores as opposed to buying online

11. Choose **References→Citations & Bibliography→Insert Citation** from the Ribbon.

12. Choose **Add New Source** from the drop-down menu to open the Create Source dialog box.

13. Follow these steps to create the new source to insert as the citation:

Ⓐ Choose **Web Site** from the Type of Source drop-down menu.

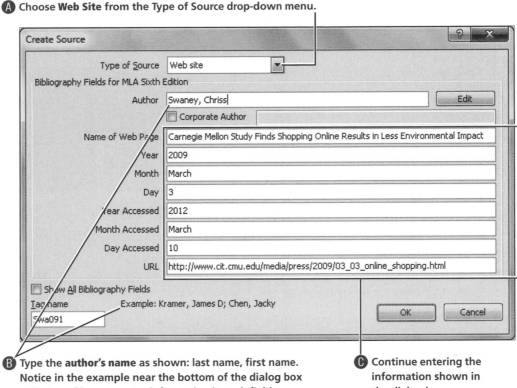

Ⓑ Type the **author's name** as shown: last name, first name. Notice in the example near the bottom of the dialog box a display of how to enter information in each field.

Ⓒ Continue entering the information shown in the dialog box.

14. When finished, click **OK**.
Notice the author's last name has been inserted automatically as the name of the citation enclosed in parentheses.

Insert a Citation Placeholder

15. Position the **insertion point** at the end of the last line of the document but before the period.

> • A truck delivering numerous packages along its way is the largest environmental savings, as it
>
> uses less energy per package than if the consumers had driven to the shops themselves|

16. **Tap** the ⌷Spacebar⌷, and then choose **References→Citations & Bibliography→Insert Citation** from the Ribbon.

17. Follow these steps to create a placeholder for a citation named *Fowler:*

Ⓐ Choose **Add New Placeholder** from the drop-down menu to open the Placeholder Name dialog box. ————

Placeholder Name

Type the tag name of the source. You can add more information to this source later by clicking Edit in the Source Manager.

Fowler| ————————

Ⓑ Type **Fowler** in the name box, and click **OK**.

Add New Source...

Add New Placeholder...

OK   Cancel

18. Save 💾 the document, and then continue with the next topic.

Editing and Formatting Footnotes

Video Lesson   labyrinthelab.com/videos

You can edit footnote text directly in the footnote area. In addition to editing the text of a footnote, you can also do the following:

- **Reposition**—You can change the position of a footnote reference mark in the main part of the document by dragging it to another location.

- **Format**—You can change various formatting features of footnotes. For example, you can change the numbering scheme, the starting number, or even replace a footnote number with a special symbol.

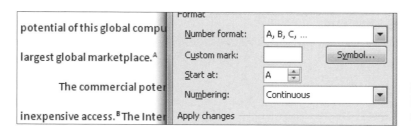

potential of this global compu

largest global marketplace.ᴬ

The commercial pote

inexpensive access.ᴮ The Inte

Format

Number format: | A, B, C, ...

Custom mark: | | Symbol...

Start at: | A

Numbering: | Continuous

Apply changes

In this example, uppercase letters replace the normal numbering for this footnote.

Changing the Text Style of a Footnote

Word's default style for the footnote text does not meet the requirements of the MLA documentation style. Therefore, you need to change the formatting if you want to be in compliance with MLA. MLA requirements state the text should be the same formatting as the regular text in the document; that is, double-spaced and with first line indented. You can also change the number format and location for the footnotes using the Footnote and Endnote dialog box.

¹ This is the opinion of many business lea
² This is true in the United States, but son
service providers.
³ These factors depend upon the capabili

This is an example of Word's default
formatting of footnotes; it is single-
spaced and a smaller font size than
the other text in the document.

¹ This is the opinion of many business l

² This is true in the United States, but s

competition among Internet service providers

³ These factors depend upon the capal

This is an example after the footnote formatting has been
changed to the same format as the rest of the document.
Notice the first line of text is indented, is double-spaced,
and is the same font size as the rest of the document.

Editing a Citation

Once you insert a placeholder for a citation or create a source, you can edit the information in
the Edit Source dialog box. You choose what type of source you are using, for example, a book,
an article, a website, and so forth. You then edit all the pertinent information about the source,
such as author's name, document name, and website address. The default citation is the
author's last name; however, you could choose to suppress it and instead show the name of
the web page.

The author's name is entered
last name, first name.

You choose the type of source from this list,
for example, a book, article, or website.

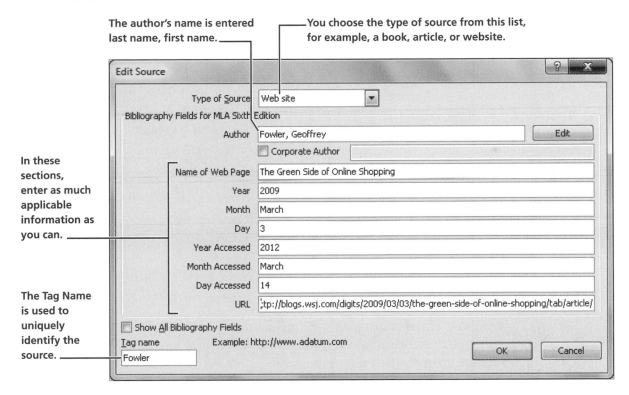

In these
sections,
enter as much
applicable
information as
you can.

The Tag Name
is used to
uniquely
identify the
source.

Task	Procedure
Insert a footnote	■ Choose References→Footnotes→Insert Footnote from the Ribbon.
Navigate to footnotes	■ Choose References→Footnotes→Next Footnote from the Ribbon.
Edit footnotes in Print Layout View	■ Edit in the designated area at the bottom of the page.
Format a footnote	■ Choose References→Footnotes from the Ribbon. ■ Click the dialog box launcher ⬚ to access the Footnote and Endnote dialog box. ■ Make the desired formatting changes.
Change the style of footnote text	■ Select the footnote text. ■ Make the desired text and paragraph style changes.
Delete a footnote	■ Select the footnote number in the document area and tap the [Delete] key. The note text associated with the mark is deleted from the footnote area simultaneously.
Insert a citation	■ Choose References→Citations & Bibliography→Insert Citation from the Ribbon. ■ Choose Add New Source to open the Create Source dialog box. ■ Enter data in the Create Source dialog box and click OK.
Edit a citation source	■ Click on the citation in the document. ■ Click the down arrow to the right of the citation. ■ Choose Edit Source from the drop-down menu. ■ Make the desired changes in the dialog box and click OK.
Edit a citation	■ Click on the citation in the document. ■ Click the down arrow to the right of the citation. ■ Choose Edit Citation from the drop-down menu. ■ Make the desired changes in the dialog box and click OK.

DEVELOP YOUR SKILLS 8.2.2

Format, Edit, and Delete Footnotes and Citations

In this exercise, you will practice formatting, editing, and deleting footnotes and citations.

Format Footnotes

1. Position the **insertion point** at the beginning of the second paragraph on the first page and scroll, if necessary, so you can see the three footnote indicators and the footnote text at the bottom of the first page.

2. Choose **References→Footnotes→dialog box launcher** to display the Footnote and Endnote dialog box.

3. Choose **Footnotes** in the Location area at the top of the dialog box.

4. Click the Number Format drop-down arrow, and choose **A, B, C…** from the list.

5. Click the **Apply** button.
Notice that the footnote numbers change to alphabetic characters. You use the same technique to change the format of endnotes.

6. Click the **Undo** ↩ button to return the footnote formatting to numbers.

7. Select the **three footnotes** at the bottom of the page.

8. Follow these steps to format the footnotes:
   - Change the line spacing to **double-space**.
   - Change the font size to **11**.
   - If necessary, display the ruler, and then drag the top triangle to **indent** the first lines **one-half inch**.

Delete a Footnote

9. Follow these steps to delete a footnote:

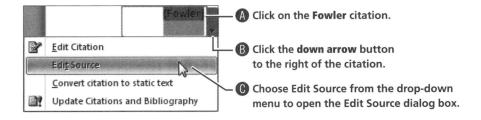

Ⓐ Select the **marker** by dragging the mouse pointer over it.

Ⓑ **Tap** [Delete] to remove the marker. The footnote indicator and the footnote text are removed. Notice also that the remaining footnotes have been renumbered.

10. Click the **Undo** ↩ button to replace the footnote indicator and its text.

Edit a Footnote

11. Position the **insertion point** between the last word and the period of the first footnote.

12. **Tap** the [Spacebar] and type **and economists**.

Edit a Citation and a Source

13. Scroll to **page 2** to view the Fowler citation.

14. Follow these steps to open the Edit Source dialog box:

Ⓐ Click on the **Fowler** citation.

Ⓑ Click the **down arrow** button to the right of the citation.

Ⓒ Choose Edit Source from the drop-down menu to open the Edit Source dialog box.

15. Follow these steps to edit the source information for the Fowler citation:

Ⓐ Choose **Web Site** for the source type.

Ⓑ Type **Fowler, Geoffrey** for the author's name.

Ⓒ Enter the remaining data shown in the illustration.

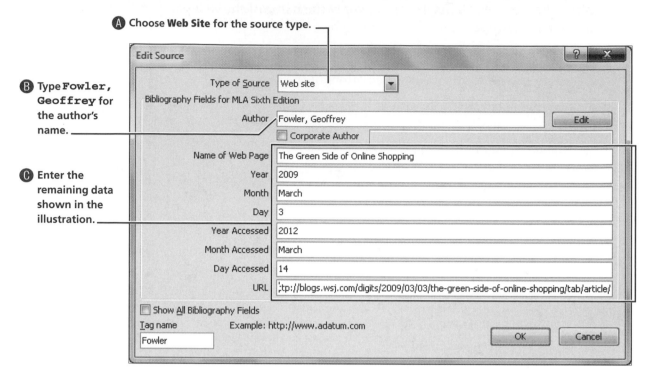

16. Click **OK** to close the Edit Source dialog box.

17. Click **Yes** if a message box appears asking if you want to update the master list and the current document.

18. **Save** 💾 the file, and leave it **open** for the next topic.

8.3 Working with Bibliographies

Video Lesson   labyrinthelab.com/videos

A bibliography is a list of all the sources that were referred to in preparation of the document. This list may be called different things depending on which documentation style you are using. MLA requires a separate page at the end of the document titled Works Cited. The Works Cited page is an alphabetical listing of all sources actually referred to in citations in the document.

Changing the Bibliography Style

You choose the documentation style from the Style drop-down menu in the Citations & Bibliography group on the References tab. Different documentation styles require different bibliography formatting; therefore, the Create Source dialog box will contain different fields, depending on which documentation style is selected in the Citations & Bibliography group. One example of this is the requirement difference for a website citation for MLA versus APA documentation style. The APA style requires the name of the web page and the name of the website, whereas the MLA style requires only the name of the web page. The source data entered is used later to create the bibliography.

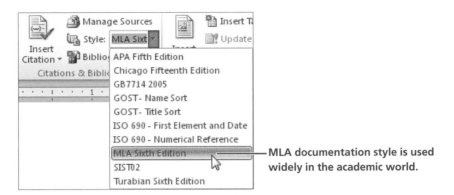

MLA documentation style is used widely in the academic world.

Creating a Bibliography

The bibliography list is created according to the document style you selected from the Style menu. It picks up the information you entered in the Create Source dialog box and creates the list with the correct punctuation in the bibliography. However, certain formatting requirements such as the title location and the double-spacing between paragraphs are not Microsoft defaults and must be done separately.

The Bibliography button in the Citations & Bibliography group on the References tab contains two built-in options: Bibliography and Works Cited. You can choose either of these; however, the paragraph formatting may or may not meet the requirements of the document style you chose. For example, the Works Cited option for the MLA style does not format the title, the paragraph spacing, or the line spacing correctly. Thus, it is advised that you type the title at the top-center of the page and then use the Insert Bibliography command rather than one of the built-in options.

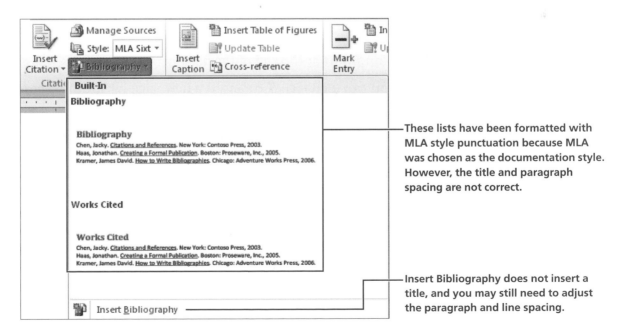

These lists have been formatted with MLA style punctuation because MLA was chosen as the documentation style. However, the title and paragraph spacing are not correct.

Insert Bibliography does not insert a title, and you may still need to adjust the paragraph and line spacing.

Creating an Alphabetic List of Citations

In a document using the MLA documentation style, the bibliography is titled Works Cited. The MLA Works Cited page has specific requirements.

┌─Title is centered one inch from the top of the paper and
│ created on a separate page at the end of the document.

── Works Cited

Fowler, Geoffrey. The Green Side of Online Shopping. 3 March 2009. 14 March 2012

        <http://blogs.wsj.com/digits/2009/03/03/the-green-side-of-online-shopping/tab/article/>.

Swaney, Chriss. Carnegie Mellon Study Finds Shopping Online Results in Less Environmental Impact. 3 March 2009.

        10 March 2012 <http://www.cit.cmu.edu/media/press/2009/03_03_online_shopping.html>.

└─Sources are listed in alphabetical order no matter what order they appear in
throughout the document. Paragraphs are double-spaced and use a hanging indent.

Updating a Bibliography

When you edit the citation source or add a new one, you can easily update the bibliography list using the Update Field command on the drop-down menu when you right-click anywhere on the list. When you use the Update Field command, it reformats the list to single-spacing again; thus, you must remember to change it to double-spacing.

DEVELOP YOUR SKILLS 8.3.1

Create a Bibliography

In this exercise, you will create a bibliography for the citations in the document. You will title the page as Works Cited since the lesson is following the MLA documentation style. Finally, you will edit an existing citation, update the bibliography list, and format the paragraphs with double-spacing.

Create a New Page and Add the Title

1. Position the **insertion point** at the end of the document.

2. **Tap** Enter twice, and **tap** Ctrl + Enter to insert a new page for the bibliography that you will insert in the next section of the exercise.

3. Choose **Home→Paragraph→Center** ≣ from the Ribbon to center the insertion point. Type **Works Cited** and **tap** Enter.

Insert the Bibliography List

4. Choose **References→Citations & Bibliography→Bibliography** 📑 from the Ribbon.

5. Choose **Insert Bibliography** from the drop-down menu.

Update a Bibliography

6. **Scroll up** and click on the **Fowler** citation at the bottom of the second page and click the **down arrow** on the right of it.

7. Open the **Edit Source** dialog box, change the Day Accessed to **10**, and then click **OK**.

8. **Scroll down** the Works Cited page, and notice nothing has changed yet in the list.

9. Follow these steps to update the bibliography:

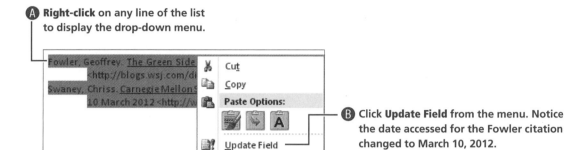

A **Right-click** on any line of the list to display the drop-down menu.

B Click **Update Field** from the menu. Notice the date accessed for the Fowler citation changed to March 10, 2012.

Notice after you use the Update Field command, the list is single-spaced; thus, you must manually double-space between paragraphs.

Format the List

10. Using the margin area, select the **bibliography list** (do not select the title).

11. Choose **Home→Paragraph→Line and Paragraph Spacing** from the Ribbon.

12. Choose **2.0** from the drop-down menu to double-space the selected list.

13. **Save** the document and continue with the next topic.

8.4 Introducing Headers and Footers

Video Lesson labyrinthelab.com/videos

There is a header area and a footer area at the top and bottom of every page in a document, above and below the margins. You can place text, page number codes, date codes, graphics, and other items in the header and footer areas. When you enter information in these areas, it is replicated on every page of the document, or you can specify different headers and footers for each section of a document.

You choose the Header or Footer command from the Header and Footer group on the Insert tab of the Ribbon. Word offers a variety of header and footer formatting styles that you can choose from the menu.

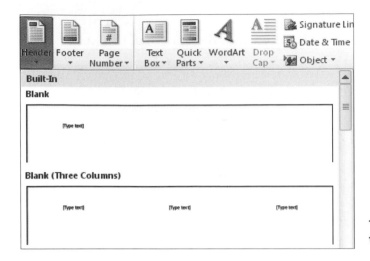

These are just two examples of the many built-in header styles.

If you wish to create your own header or footer from scratch, you can choose the Edit Header or Edit Footer commands from the Header or Footer menu, and then type and format the header or footer.

Formatting Headers and Footers

The Design tab under Header and Footer Tools on the Ribbon provides many options for formatting a header or footer. For example, you can format page numbers as alphabetic characters or Roman Numerals using the Format Page Numbers command.

Using the Insert group on the same tab, you can insert date and time codes, documents such as the author or company name, or fields such as the document's filename and path.

The Header and Footer Design contextual tab replaces the Header and Footer Custom Dialog Box found in previous versions of Word.

QUICK REFERENCE	WORKING WITH HEADERS AND FOOTERS
Task	**Procedure**
Create a header/ footer	■ Choose Insert→Header & Footer→Header/Footer from the Ribbon. ■ Choose a built-in header/footer style. *or* ■ Choose Edit Header/Footer from the menu and create your own.
Delete a header/ footer	■ Choose Insert→Header & Footer→Header/Footer from the Ribbon. ■ Choose Remove Header/Footer from the menu.
Format page numbers	■ Choose Header and Footer Tools→Design→Header and Footer→Page Number from the Ribbon. ■ Choose Format Page Numbers from the menu. ■ Choose the desired number format in the Page Number Format dialog box. ■ Click OK.
Insert a date and time code	■ Choose Header and Footer Tools→Design→Insert→Date & Time from the Ribbon. ■ Choose the desired date format in the Date and Time dialog box. ■ Click OK.

Add a Header to the Report

In this exercise, you will add a page number and the author's name to the report. As specified in the MLA guidelines, the page number and name must be right-aligned at the top of the page.

1. Position the **insertion point** at the top of the document.

2. Choose **Insert→Header & Footer→Page Number** [#] from the Ribbon.

3. Choose **Top of Page** from the menu, and then choose **Plain Number 3** from the gallery.
   This places page number 1 right-aligned in the header area. Now you will add the writer's name.

4. Choose **Insert→Header & Footer→Header** [ ] from the Ribbon.

5. Choose **Edit Header** from the bottom of the menu.
   This positions the insertion point in the page number object to the left of the number. When you are already in the Header section, steps 4 and 5 are not required; you can just begin editing. The steps are included here as reinforcement of where the command is located.

6. Type **Simpson**, and then **tap** the [Spacebar].

7. **Double-click** in the document background to close the header area and to view the header text.

8. Scroll to the top of **page 2**, and observe the header.

9. **Save** [💾] the file, and leave it **open** for the next topic.

8.5 Inserting Captions and a Table of Figures

Video Lesson labyrinthelab.com/videos

You use captions to insert text associated with figures or tables in a paper. Word then uses the captions as entries in the table of figures. Later, if you alter some of the captions, Word updates these when you regenerate the table of figures.

Inserting Captions

Word can automate or semiautomate the creation of captions for figures in a document. For example, you can standardize on the phrase *Figure x*, with Word automatically assigning a number to each caption. You can choose References→Captions→Insert Caption to open the Caption dialog box, or right-click on an object and choose Insert Caption from the drop-down menu.

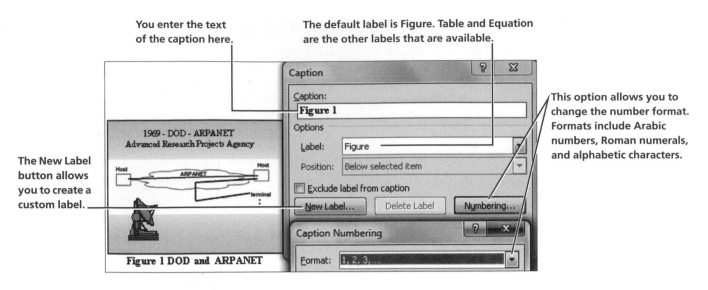

You enter the text of the caption here.

The default label is Figure. Table and Equation are the other labels that are available.

This option allows you to change the number format. Formats include Arabic numbers, Roman numerals, and alphabetic characters.

The New Label button allows you to create a custom label.

Generating a Table of Figures

A table of figures guides the reader to all tables, charts, diagrams, pictures, and other graphic elements in a document. Before creating a table of figures, you mark the figures in your document with captions.

DEVELOP YOUR SKILLS 8.5.1

Add Captions to Figures

In this exercise, you will insert a file between page 1 and 2 that contains five PowerPoint slides pasted from a presentation. You will add captions to the slides in preparation for creating a table of figures.

Insert a File

1. Position the **insertion point** after the Footnote 3 indicator at the bottom of the first page.

2. **Press** Ctrl + Enter to insert a page break.

3. Choose **Insert→Text→Object** menu ▾ from the Ribbon, and then choose **Text from File** from the menu.

4. In the Insert File dialog box, navigate to your Lesson 08 folder, choose Internet Slides, and then click the **Insert** button.

5. If necessary, choose **Home→Paragraph→Show/Hide** ¶ from the Ribbon to display formatting marks.

6. **Tap** Delete to remove any extra paragraph marks between the last paragraph of the new file inserted and the next one.

Add Captions and Edit a Caption

7. Position the **insertion point** on the first blank line below the first slide.

8. Choose **References→Captions→Insert Caption** from the Ribbon to open the Caption dialog box.

9. The Caption dialog box should match the following illustration. If *Figure 1* does not appear in the Caption text box at the top of the dialog box, follow these steps. Otherwise, go to step 11.

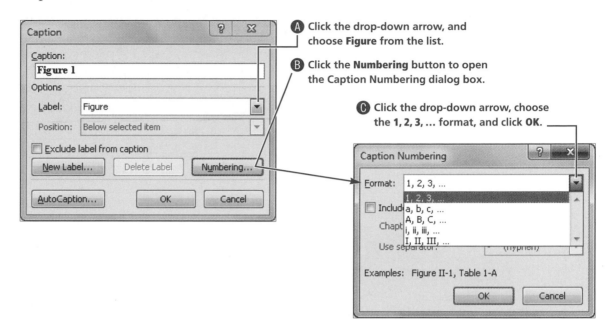

Ⓐ Click the drop-down arrow, and choose **Figure** from the list.

Ⓑ Click the **Numbering** button to open the Caption Numbering dialog box.

Ⓒ Click the drop-down arrow, choose the **1, 2, 3, ...** format, and click **OK**.

10. If necessary, position the **insertion point** to the right of *Figure 1* in the Caption text box.

11. **Tap** the ⎵Spacebar⎵, type **DOD and ARPANET**, and click **OK** to insert the caption. *Notice the caption is placed on the left margin; you will fix this problem in the next step.*

12. Choose **Home→Paragraph→Center** ≡ to center the caption.

13. Position the **insertion point** in the first blank line below the second slide.

14. Choose **References→Captions→Insert Caption** from the Ribbon to open the Caption dialog box for Figure 2.

15. **Tap** the ⎵Spacebar⎵, type **NSF**, and click **OK**.

16. **Center** ≡ the caption.

17. Add the **captions** shown in the following table and **center** them:

Slide Number	Caption Text
3	MILNET and TCP/IP
4	First Graphical Browser
5	Netscape

Edit a Caption

18. Return to **slide 2**, select *NSF*, and type **National Science Foundation** in its place.

19. Choose **Home→Paragraph→Show/Hide** ¶ from the Ribbon to turn off the formatting marks.

20. **Save** the file, and leave it **open** for the next exercise.

Inserting a Table of Figures

Video Lesson   labyrinthelab.com/videos

Academic papers often include a table of figures at the front, which guides the reader to illustrations, charts, tables, and other types of figures. This is particularly helpful in long documents. The table entries conveniently function as hyperlinks if you are reading the document online. You will create a table of figures like the one in the following illustration.

Table of Figures	
Figure 1 DOD and ARPANET	3
Figure 2 National Science Foundation	3
Figure 3 MILNET and TCP/IP	3
Figure 4 First Graphical Browser	4
Figure 5 Netscape	4

QUICK REFERENCE	CREATING CAPTIONS AND TABLES OF FIGURES
Task	**Procedure**
Insert a caption	■ Choose References→Captions→Insert Caption from the Ribbon. ■ Type the text for the caption.
Insert a table of figures	■ Choose References→Captions→Insert Table of Figures from the Ribbon. ■ Make formatting choices in the Table of Figures dialog box.
Update a table of figures	■ Right-click the table, and choose Update Field from the pop-up menu.

DEVELOP YOUR SKILLS 8.5.2
Generate a Table of Figures

In this exercise, you will generate a table of figures from the captions you inserted in the preceding exercise. You will change the numbering format of your captions, and then you will update the table to reflect the change.

Insert the Table of Figures

1. Move the **insertion point** to the top of the document, and insert a **page break**.

2. **Tap** Ctrl + Home to position the insertion point at the top of the new page, type **Table of Figures**, and **tap** Enter twice.

3. Select the **heading** you just typed, **center** ☰ it, and format it with **bold 16 pt**.

4. Place the **insertion point** in the blank line below the heading.

5. Choose **References→Captions→Insert Table of Figures** 📄 from the Ribbon.

6. Follow these steps to set up the table:

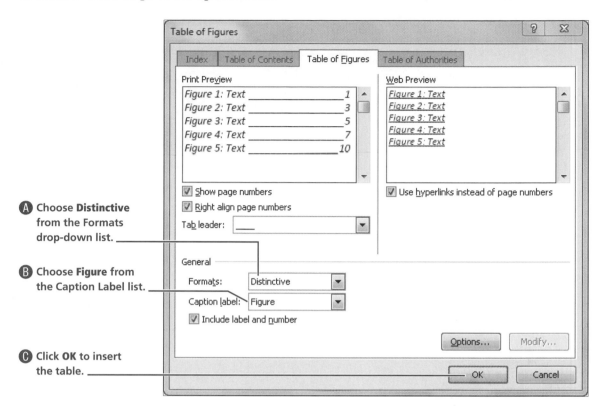

A Choose **Distinctive** from the Formats drop-down list.

B Choose **Figure** from the Caption Label list.

C Click **OK** to insert the table.

7. Position the **insertion point** on page 3 of the document.

Change the Numbering Format of the Captions

8. Choose **References→Captions→Insert Caption** 📄 from the Ribbon.

9. Click the **Numbering** button in the bottom-right corner of the dialog box, and the Caption Numbering dialog box appears.

10. Choose the **A, B, C,...** format, as shown at right, and then click **OK**.

11. Click the **Close** button in the Caption dialog box, and **scroll** through the slides. Notice that the figure numbers changed to alphabetic characters.

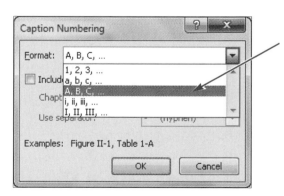

Update the Table of Figures

12. **Scroll up** to view the Table of Figures on page 1. Notice that the table is still showing the numeric figure numbers.

13. Follow these steps to update the table of figures:

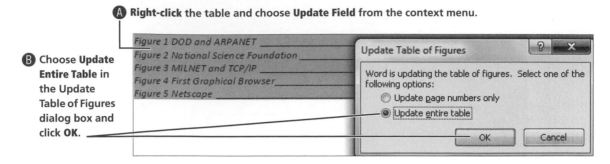

Ⓐ **Right-click** the table and choose **Update Field** from the context menu.

Ⓑ Choose **Update Entire Table** in the Update Table of Figures dialog box and click **OK**.

The table should match the following illustration.

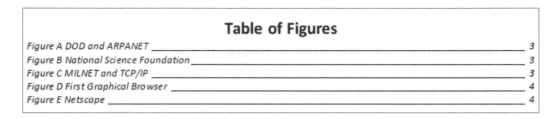

Table of Figures

Figure A DOD and ARPANET	3
Figure B National Science Foundation	3
Figure C MILNET and TCP/IP	3
Figure D First Graphical Browser	4
Figure E Netscape	4

The text switched from Figures 1–5 to Figures A–E.

14. Save 🖫 the file, and **close** it.

8.6 Working with Templates

Video Lesson labyrinthelab.com/videos

All Word documents are based on templates, which can include text, formatting, graphics, and any other objects or formats available in Word. The default Word template is named Normal, which contains one-inch margins, Calibri 11 pt font, line spacing of 1.15, and other settings. The benefit of templates is that they do not change when documents based on them change. When you start a new document based on a template, Word opens a *copy* of the template. This lets you use templates repeatedly as the basis for new documents. Word provides a variety of ready-to-use templates, and if necessary, you can modify them to suit your needs. You can also create custom templates.

Creating a Document from a Template

You choose File→New to access the Available Templates pane, from where you can use existing templates or create new custom templates. Basing a new document on a saved template can save you a lot of time since much of the formatting is already included in the template for you.

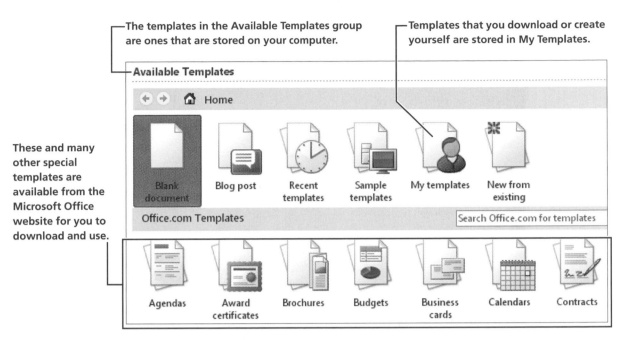

The templates in the Available Templates group are ones that are stored on your computer.

Templates that you download or create yourself are stored in My Templates.

These and many other special templates are available from the Microsoft Office website for you to download and use.

The appearance of this window may vary depending on recent actions taken here.

Saving Documents as Templates

When you create a document containing specific formatting, you can save it to use later as a template. You should save the template in the Templates folder. This is what causes your templates to appear in the My Templates folder found in the Available Templates section. You can save a template as a .dotx file type or a .dotm file type. A .dotm file is one that contains a special series of instructions, called a macro.

DEVELOP YOUR SKILLS 8.6.1
Create a Template from an Existing Document

In this exercise, you will open a copy of a report and save it as a template. The body text of the report has been removed; however, other elements are still in place, such as the cover page, the table of figures, and the double spacing. You will save time by starting new reports based on the template.

Save an Existing Document as a Template

1. **Open** My Report from the Lesson 08 folder.

2. **Scroll** through the document, and notice the elements that are still in place in the document that will be useful when you create a new report.

3. Choose **File→Save As**.

4. Click **Templates** in the left pane of the Save As dialog box.

 You may need to expand the Microsoft icon in the left pane by pointing to it and clicking its left arrow, to display the Templates folder.

5. Choose **Word Template** from the Save As Type drop-down list at the bottom of the dialog box.

6. Name the file **My Report Template**, and then click **Save**.

7. Close the template file.

Create a New Document Based on the Template

8. Choose **File→New**.

9. Follow these steps start a new document based on a template:

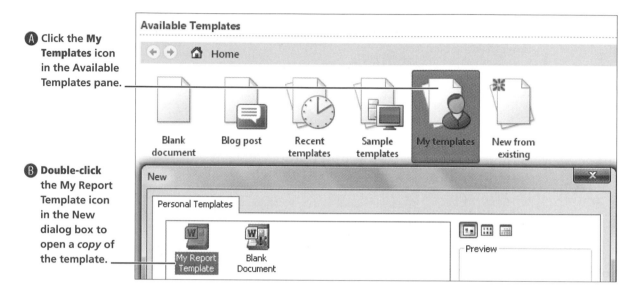

Ⓐ Click the **My Templates** icon in the Available Templates pane.

Ⓑ **Double-click** the My Report Template icon in the New dialog box to open a *copy* of the template.

Notice the title bar with the generic Document(x) name that appears at the top of the window. This indicates that this is just a regular Word document and you are not changing the actual template.

10. Scroll to **page 3**, and replace [DOCUMENT TITLE] with **The Green Life**.

11. Save 💾 the document as **Green Life** in the Lesson 08 folder, and then **close** it.

Deleting a Template

Video Lesson   labyrinthelab.com/videos

When a template is no longer useful, you may wish to delete it. Templates are easily removed from the New dialog box. It's a good idea to delete unwanted templates so the dialog box does not become too cluttered.

QUICK REFERENCE	CREATING AND DELETING TEMPLATES
Task	**Procedure**
Save an existing document as a template	▪ Choose File→Save. ▪ Click the Templates icon. ▪ Choose Word Template (*.dotx) from the Save As Type menu.
Delete a template	▪ Choose File→New. ▪ Choose My Templates from the pane on the left. ▪ Right-click the template you wish to delete. ▪ Choose Delete from the pop-up menu.

Delete a Template

In this exercise, you will delete the template you created.

1. Choose **File→New**.

2. Choose **My Templates** from the Available Templates dialog box to open the New dialog box.

3. Follow these steps to delete My Report Template:

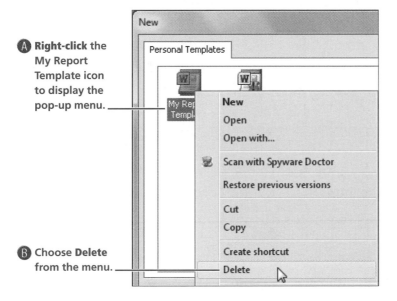

A **Right-click** the My Report Template icon to display the pop-up menu.

B Choose **Delete** from the menu.

4. When the message box appears to verify that you want to delete the template, click **Yes**. *Notice that the template was removed from the dialog box.*

5. Click **Cancel** to close the New Document dialog box.

8.7 Concepts Review

Concepts Review   labyrinthelab.com/word10

To check your knowledge of the key concepts introduced in this lesson, complete the Concepts Review quiz by going to the URL listed above. If your classroom is using Labyrinth eLab, you may complete the Concepts Review quiz from within your eLab course.

Reinforce Your Skills

Insert and Delete Footnotes

In this exercise, you will insert footnotes in a document.

1. **Open** rs-Garden Report from the Lesson 08 folder.

2. Position the **insertion point** after the word *tested* at the end of the first sentence under the *Organic Lawn Fertilizer* heading on page 2.

3. Choose **References→Footnotes→Insert Footnote** AB¹ from the Ribbon.
   The insertion point is next to the footnote number at the bottom of the page.

4. Type **Products tested by Garden Laboratories, Inc., Melville, CA** as the footnote text.
   Next you will place a footnote above the one you just inserted, which will cause renumbering of the original footnote.

5. In the *Weed Control* paragraph, position the **insertion point** to the right of the word *Rover* toward the end of the fourth line.

6. Choose **References→Footnotes→Insert Footnote** AB¹ from the Ribbon to place the next footnote marker at the bottom of the page.
   Notice that the original footnote is numbered 2.

7. Type **Products approved by the Wildlife Association of America**.

8. Position the **insertion point** at the end of the third bullet on page 3.

9. Insert a footnote marker, and type **Manufacturer's warranty is 60 days**.

10. Position the **insertion point** after the words *Mighty Mulcher* on the last page.

11. Insert a footnote marker, and type the footnote **Extended manufacturer's warranty available**.
    Next you will delete the footnote next to Rover *in the* Weed Control *paragraph.*

Delete a Footnote

12. Return to **page 2**, and **select** the footnote marker next to *Rover* in the *Weed Control* paragraph.

13. **Tap** Delete to remove the marker.

14. **Scroll** to the bottom of the page, and notice that the footnote is gone and the second footnote renumbered to 1.

15. **Scroll** through the other pages, and observe that renumbering took place.

16. **Save** 💾 the file, and **close** it.

Insert Headers and Footers

In this exercise, you will add headers and footers to a document you prepared as a handout for your meeting presentation. You will use the Edit Header command to add your header, and then you will use one of Word's predesigned footers to add page numbers to your document. You will also format the header and footer text.

Add a Header

1. **Open** rs-Options from the Lesson 08 folder.

2. Choose **Insert→Header & Footer→Header** 📄 from the Ribbon.

3. Choose **Edit Header** from the bottom of the menu.

4. Type **Options and Swaps Presentation** at the header's left margin.

5. **Tap** Tab twice to right-align the insertion point, and then type **GRCC Chapter Meeting**.

6. Select the header text and use the Mini Toolbar to change the font size to **9**.

7. **Double-click** in the body of the document to close the header area.

Add a Footer

8. Choose **Insert→Header & Footer→Footer** 📄 from the Ribbon.

9. **Scroll down** the list of preformatted footers, and choose **Alphabet** from the menu to insert page numbers in your document.

10. Replace [Type Text] with **Presented by: [Your Name]**.

11. Select the **footer** text, including the page number, and use the Mini Toolbar to change the font to **9 pt italics**.

12. **Double-click** in the body of the document to close the footer area.

13. **Scroll** through the document, and observe your headers and footers.

14. **Save** 💾 the file, and **close** it.

Insert Captions and a Table of Figures

In this exercise, you will add captions to the pictures in a document, and then you will generate a table of figures from the captions.

Insert Captions

1. **Open** rs-Rose Catalog from the Lesson 08 folder.

2. Scroll to **page 3** of the document, and position the **insertion point** on the blank line below the first rose picture.

3. Choose **References→Captions→Insert Caption** 🖼 from the Ribbon to open the Caption dialog box.

4. If Figure 1 appears in the Caption text box, continue with the next step. Otherwise, click the **numbering** button, choose **1, 2, 3,…** from the Format drop-down list, and click **OK**.

5. Make sure the **insertion point** is to the right of *Figure 1* in the Caption text box.

6. **Tap** the Spacebar, type **Floribunda**, and click **OK**.

7. Repeat this technique to enter **captions** below the next three pictures. Use the following captions:

   - **Glorious**
   - **Moondance**
   - **Heaven on Earth**

Generate the Table of Figures

8. Go to **page 2**, and position the **insertion point** on the second blank line below the Table of Figures heading.

9. Choose **References→Captions→Insert Table of Figures** 🖼 from the Ribbon.

10. Choose **Formal** from the list of formats to match the following illustration.

Table of Figures
FIGURE 1 FLORIBUNDA...3
FIGURE 2 GLORIOUS..3
FIGURE 3 MOONDANCE..3
FIGURE 4 HEAVEN ON EARTH...3

11. Click **OK** to insert the Table of Figures.

12. **Save** 💾 the file, and **close** it.

Create a Template from an Existing Document

In this exercise, you will open a document and save it as a template. You will then open a copy of the template, and finally you will delete the template.

1. **Open** rs-Rose Sales from the Lesson 08 folder.

2. Choose **File→Save As**.

3. Click the **Templates** icon in the left pane of the Save As dialog box to switch to the Templates folder.

4. Choose **Word Template** from the Save As Type drop-down list at the bottom of the dialog box.

5. Name the file **rs-My Rose Template**.

6. Click the **Save** button.

7. **Close** the template.

Open a Copy of the Template

8. Choose **File→New**.

9. Choose **My Templates** from Available Templates to open the New dialog box.

10. **Double-click** the rs-My Rose Template icon to open a copy of the template. *Notice the generic Document(x) name in the title bar.*

11. **Close** the document without saving.

Delete a Template

12. Choose **File→New**.

13. Choose **My Templates** from Available Templates to open the New dialog box.

14. **Right-click** the rs-My Rose Template icon, and choose **Delete** from the menu.

15. When the message box appears, click **Yes** to complete the deletion.

16. Click **Cancel** to close the New dialog box.

Apply Your Skills

Create Captions and a Table of Figures

In this exercise, you will open a real estate brochure and place captions below the pictures of the houses. Then you will generate a table of figures that lists the captions and their associated page numbers.

Add the Captions

1. **Open** as-RE Brochure from the Lesson 08 folder.

2. Create the following **captions** for each house picture in the brochure, but this time try a different method. Instead of going to the Ribbon to access the Insert Caption command, **right-click** on the picture and choose **Insert Caption** from the pop-up menu.

   Figure 1 **Pleasant Valley charming cottage**

   Figure 2 **Burgundy Valley appealing updated home**

   Figure 3 **Pleasant Valley cottage with delightful garden**

   Figure 4 **Kensington two-story charmer**

   Figure 5 **Lakeville waterfront cottage with dock**

3. **Scroll up** and position the **insertion point** at the bottom of page 1 at about the 6 ½-inch mark on the ruler, as shown in the following illustration.

4. **Tap** Ctrl + Enter to insert a page break.

5. Type **Table of Figures** and tap Enter.

6. Reduce the size of the heading to **14 pt**.

Generate the Table of Figures

7. Position the **insertion point** on the first blank line below the heading.

8. Choose **References→Captions→Insert Table of Figures** 🔲 from the Ribbon.

9. Choose the **Distinctive** format, and click **OK** to generate the table.
   Next you will modify one of the captions and then regenerate the table.

10. Go to the **Figure 2** caption and change *appealing* to `attractive`.

11. Scroll down to the **Figure 4** caption and insert the word `colonial` before the word *charmer*.

12. Return to the table, and **right-click** it to view the pop-up menu.

13. Choose **Update Field** from the menu, choose **Update Entire Table** in the Update Table of Figures dialog box, and then click **OK**.
   That updates the table with the Figure 2 edit you just made.

14. **Save** 💾 the file, and **close** it.

Create a Research Paper with Citations and a Bibliography

Most English and humanities classes follow the method for writing research papers dictated in the MLA handbook. Various academic disciplines use their own editorial guidelines for citing resources in research papers. Following is a list of organizations that sponsor style manuals.

- *Modern Language Association*
  http://www.mla.org
- *Council of Science Editors*
  http://www.councilscienceeditors.org
- *Linguistic Society of America*
  http://www.lsadc.org/

In this exercise, you will visit these websites (or websites of your choice with related topics) and locate the mission statement (or an overview statement) on each site. You will then copy a paragraph from each mission statement and paste it in your research paper. Then you will insert a citation for each paragraph, citing the web page of the organization in the footnote. (Results may vary due to the changing nature of the Internet.)

1. Start a **new** document, and **format** it according to the MLA guidelines outlined at the beginning of this lesson.

2. Add a **right-aligned header** with your last name and the page number.

3. **Type** the student name, professor, course, and date at the top of the first page. The student name is your name, the professor is **Professor Higgins**, and the course is **Humanities 101**. Use today's date.

4. Type **Style Guide Research** as the title of the paper.

5. Use the **URLs** provided above to visit the websites of the organizations listed (or similar organizations).

6. **Copy** a paragraph from the mission statement or overview statement of each site, and paste it into your paper.

7. **Format** the text according to your preferences but within the MLA guidelines.

8. Insert a **citation** at the end of each paragraph, and add the required **source data** from each web page.

9. Create a **new page** at the end of the document.

10. **Center** and type **Works Cited** as the title for the new page.

11. Insert a **bibliography** (do not use the built-in Bibliography or Works Cited option).

12. **Double-space** the lines in the bibliography list.

13. **Save** 🖫 the file in the Lesson 08 folder as **as–Style Research** and **close** it.

Critical Thinking & Work-Readiness Skills

In the course of working through the following Microsoft Office-based Critical Thinking exercises, you will also be utilizing various work-readiness skills, some of which are listed next to each exercise. Go to labyrinthelab.com/ workreadiness to learn more about the work-readiness skills.

8.1 Add Footnotes, Citations, Headers, and Footers

Jordan Stewart, a college intern working at Green Clean, has been asked to research the environmental benefits of using washable fabric napkins rather than disposable paper napkins. Her research, which was assigned by her professor, will be shared with Green Clean clients as a community service. Open the ct-Napkin Research file (Lesson 08 folder) and save a copy of it as **ct-Napkin Research Footnotes**. Insert an appropriate header, your name, your teacher's name, your course, and today's date, all formatted to MLA specifications. Format the rest of the document text with a Calibri 11 pt font. Make up three humorous footnotes with citations and add a header and footer. Save your changes.

WORK-READINESS SKILLS APPLIED

- Using computers to process information
- Organizing and maintaining information
- Thinking creatively

8.2 Work with Figures and Captions

Start with the ct-Napkin Research Footnotes document you created in the previous exercise and save a copy of it with the name **ct-Napkin Figures** to your Lesson 08 folder. Add creative captions to the two figures and create a table of figures. Insert a cover page with appropriate text and formatting. Remember, this is a research paper that will be shared with customers, so make sure it is customer appropriate. Save your changes. If working in a group, discuss what may be considered "customer appropriate" and not. If working alone, type your answers in a Word document named **ct-Questions** saved to your Lesson 08 folder.

WORK-READINESS SKILLS APPLIED

- Serving clients/ customers
- Making decisions
- Participating as a member of a team (or Writing)

8.3 Create a Template and add a Bibliography

Open the ct-Napkin Figures document you created in the previous exercise. Take one last look to verify proper MLA formatting and a professional cover page. Save it as a template to Word's Templates folder as **Research Paper [First Last] Template** (substitute your actual first and last name). Create a new document based on the template you just created and save it to your Lesson 08 folder as **ct-Child Page**. Add a bibliography page to the end of the document (there is no need to fill it in). Save your changes. If working in a group, brainstorm scenarios in which having a predesigned template can be helpful. If working alone, type your answers in a Word document named **ct-Questions2** saved to your Lesson 08 folder.

WORK-READINESS SKILLS APPLIED

- Showing responsibility
- Selecting technology
- Participating as a member of a team

Creating a Promotional Brochure

LESSON OUTLINE

LEARNING OBJECTIVES

After studying this lesson, you will be able to:

- Use Shapes to add graphic interest
- Insert and edit pictures
- Work with SmartArt graphics
- Add page borders and background page color

In this lesson, you will learn to add graphic elements, such as Shapes, pictures, and SmartArt to your document, and then you will use Word's galleries to format these graphic images. Finally, you will format the page background with page color and a page border.

Promoting an Ergonomics Seminar

Josh DeLeone owns Ergonomic Office Solutions. He has called upon his old buddy, Tommy Choi, owner of Green Clean, with an idea to create a presentation about the benefits of using ergonomic equipment. He believes using Tommy's database of customers would be a great place to launch his seminar. He knows Tommy's customer base is already interested in the environment, and he believes those same customers would be interested in taking care of their ergonomic health.

Josh decides he will create a brochure, have Tommy review a draft of it, and then mail it to local businesses to promote this seminar and, thereby, spark interest in the ergonomic office furniture and computer equipment he sells. Josh uses product pictures as well as Word's Shapes and SmartArt to create a brochure that is both informative and visually appealing.

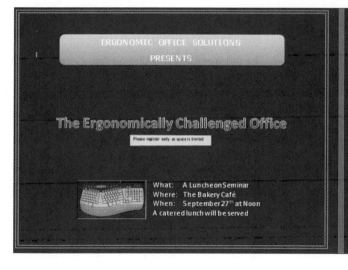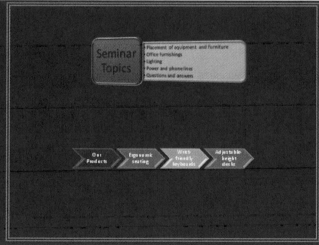

9.1 Working with Shapes

Video Lesson labyrinthelab.com/videos

Word has a large gallery of graphic shapes that you can insert into your documents. Shapes include lines; text boxes; basic shapes such as rectangles, ovals, and triangles; special shapes such as arrows, stars, callouts, and banners; and many others. They can add interest to documents such as flyers, brochures, and other graphical documents. You can also type text in most shapes.

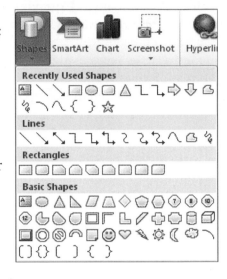

Shapes are located in the Illustrations group on the Insert tab of the Ribbon. They are found in a gallery similar to other galleries you have worked with.

You insert Shapes by choosing the desired Shape in the gallery. When the mouse pointer is in the document, it changes to a crosshair, which you click or drag in the document to create the Shape.

Rotating, Resizing, and Moving Shapes

Clicking a Shape displays the handles, which are similar to handles you've seen on clip art. If the handles are not visible, clicking the object displays them. You can move, resize, or rotate a Shape only when the handles are visible. You can insert a perfect square or circle in one of two ways: by choosing the rectangle or oval tool and clicking in the document, or by holding down the Shift key while drawing the shape.

When you place the mouse pointer on the Rotate handle, the pointer changes to a circular arrow. You can then drag left or right to rotate the object.

Position the mouse pointer on a handle, and it changes to a double-headed arrow; then you can drag to resize the object. If you hold the [Shift] **key when you drag a corner handle, the object maintains its original proportions. A square remains a square, for example.**

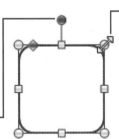

When you position the mouse pointer on the border of the selected Shape, the Move handle (four-headed arrow) indicates that you can now drag to move the Shape.

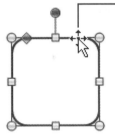

Adding and Formatting Text in Shapes

You can add text to the Shapes you draw. This can be handy if, for example, you want to create a flyer announcing an event. You can right-click a selected Shape and choose the option to add text from the pop-up menu. Alternatively, you can choose the Edit Text button in the Insert Shapes group on the Format tab of the Ribbon. Both options place the insertion point inside the drawn Shape, ready for you to type your text. Text is automatically centered both horizontally and vertically, and wraps within a shape as you type.

Selecting a Shape by the border selects all the text inside the Shape; however, it does not highlight the text, as Word normally does when you select text. You can then make character formatting changes, which will affect all of the text. If you wish to format only a portion of the text, you must drag to select it.

Formatting Shapes

When a Shape is selected, Word provides a contextual Format tab, which contains many tools you can use to add color and pizzazz to the Shape, including Shape Styles, Shadow Effects, and 3-D Effects. The Format tab also has its own Insert Shapes gallery containing the same shapes as the Shapes gallery located in the Illustrations group on the Insert tab. When multiple shapes are selected, you can align, resize, or move them.

QUICK REFERENCE	WORKING WITH SHAPES
Task	**Procedure**
Insert a perfect square	■ Choose the rectangle Shape from the Shapes gallery. ■ Click in the document. *or* ■ Hold the Shift key while dragging in the document.
Insert a perfect circle	■ Choose the oval Shape from the Shapes gallery. ■ Click in the document. *or* ■ Hold the Shift key while dragging in the document.
Maintain an object's proportions	■ Hold the Shift key while dragging a corner handle to resize.
Type text within a Shape	■ Select the Shape. ■ Begin typing.
Selecting multiple Shapes	■ Hold the Shift key down, and click on each object.
Align multiple objects	■ Select the objects using the Shift key. ■ Choose Format→Arrange→Align from the Ribbon. ■ Choose the desired alignment.
Move an object	■ Select the object. ■ Position the mouse pointer on a border to display the Move handle. ■ Drag the object to the desired location.

DEVELOP YOUR SKILLS 9.1.1
Draw Shapes and Insert Graphic Objects

In this exercise, you will draw Shapes and add text to them, and then you will insert and format WordArt and a picture into your brochure. First you will change the Theme to Office.

1. **Open** the Promo Brochure document from the Lesson 09 folder.

Change the Theme

2. Choose **Page Layout→Themes→Themes** [Aa] from the Ribbon, and then choose **Office** from the menu.
The change of Theme won't be apparent until you enter more content into your document.

Draw a Shape

First you will experiment with a Shape, and then you will insert the Shape that you will use for your brochure.

3. Choose **Insert→Illustrations→Shapes** 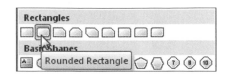 from the Ribbon to display the Shapes gallery.

4. Choose the **rounded rectangle** from the **Rectangles** section of the gallery, as shown in the following illustration.

5. **Click and drag** in the document to draw a rounded rectangle.
   Notice the rectangle shape is filled with a color; that's because you applied a Theme to this document, and themes include fill colors for shapes.

6. Choose **Format→Insert Shapes** from the Ribbon, and then click the **rounded rectangle**.

7. **Hold** the ⎵Shift⎵ key and drag to draw a rounded rectangle that's larger than the last one.
   Notice this time you drew a perfect square with rounded corners instead of a rectangle even though you started with the same Shape. This happened because you held down the ⎵Shift⎵ key while drawing.

8. Make sure the **Shape** is selected (displaying handles), and then take a moment to practice resizing it using the handles.

9. Use the **Rotate** handle at the top of one of the Shapes to rotate it.

Delete the Practice Shapes

You must select a Shape before you can delete it.

10. Click one of the **Shapes** to display the handles, and then **press and hold** the ⎵Shift⎵ key and select the other **Shape**.

 Holding the ⎵Shift⎵ key allows you to select multiple Shapes at once, and then you can delete, move, or format them all at once.

11. **Tap** ⎵Delete⎵ to remove both of the Shapes.

Draw a Shape for Your Brochure

12. If necessary, click the **View Ruler** button at the top of the vertical scroll bar to display the Ruler.
    The Ruler will be helpful in sizing your Shape.

13. Choose **Insert→Illustrations→Shapes** 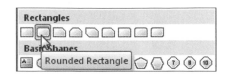 from the Ribbon.

14. Choose the **rounded rectangle** from the **Shapes** gallery, and draw a long narrow rectangle at the top margin that spans across the page. It should be about 1 inch high.

Remember, the Move handle appears when you place the mouse pointer on the border of a selected Shape. You press and hold down the mouse button, and then drag to move the Shape.

15. Use the **Move** handle to practice moving the shape around, placing it back in its original position when you are finished.

Add Text to the Shape

16. Make sure the **Shape** is still selected.

17. Tap ⌈Caps Lock⌋, begin typing **ERGONOMIC OFFICE SOLUTIONS**, tap ⌈Enter⌋, and then type **PRESENTS**.
Notice that the text was automatically centered in the Shape.

Format the Text

18. Click the **border** of the Shape.

Selecting a Shape by the border selects everything inside the Shape as well. Thus, the text in the Shape is selected, although it is not highlighted.

19. Choose **Home→Font→Font menu** from the Ribbon, and then choose **Tahoma** from the Font list.

20. Keep the **Shape** selected, and apply **bold 22 pt** font.
You may need to drag a resizing handle if your drawn shape is not big enough to display the larger text.

Format the Shape

Next, you will use the Shape Styles gallery to format the Shape. This gallery behaves like other galleries you have used.

21. Make sure the object is selected so the contextual **Format** tab is available.

22. Choose **Format→Shape Styles** from the Ribbon.

23. Follow these steps to format the Shape:

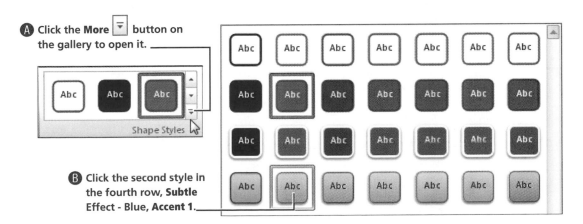

Ⓐ Click the **More** ⌄ button on the gallery to open it.

Ⓑ Click the second style in the fourth row, **Subtle Effect - Blue, Accent 1.**

Add and Align Objects

Next, you will add another object and then center it.

24. Click in the document under the **rectangle**, and choose **Insert→Text→WordArt** from the Ribbon.

25. Choose the fourth style in the fourth row, **Gradient Fill – Blue, Accent 1, Outline – White**, and then type **The Ergonomically Challenged Office**.

26. Position the **mouse pointer** on the bottom edge of the WordArt text box, and **drag** it down about **two inches** below the rectangle. You can use the illustration at the end of the exercise as a guide if you wish.

Don't worry about centering it under the object at the top of the document; you will align the objects in the next steps.

27. Follow these steps to select multiple objects:

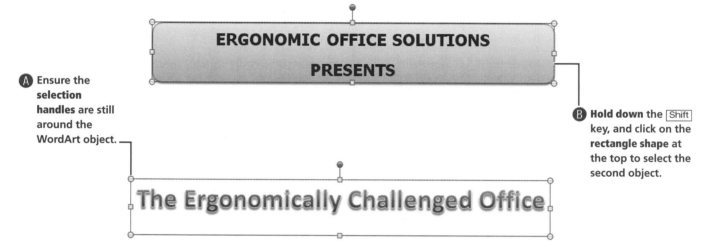

A Ensure the **selection handles** are still around the WordArt object.

B **Hold down** the [Shift] key, and click on the **rectangle shape** at the top to select the second object.

28. Make sure the contextual **Format** tab is activated on the Ribbon.

29. Follow these steps to center the two objects:

A Choose the **Drawing Tools→Format→Arrange→** **Align** button.

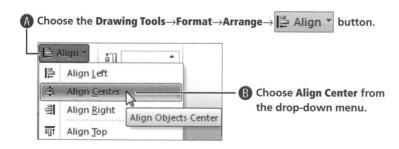

B Choose **Align Center** from the drop-down menu.

30. Position the **mouse pointer** on either of the selected objects, and then **drag** them toward the center of the page, between the margins.

Notice that because both objects are selected, they both move at the same time.

31. Click on a **blank area** of the document to deselect the objects.

Insert a Picture in the Brochure

32. Scroll down, and click in the **left cell** of the table.

33. Choose **Insert→Illustrations→Picture** from the Ribbon.

34. Navigate to the Lesson 09 folder, and **double-click** the Keyboard picture file to insert it.

35. Using the **left margin** area, click to select the **table row**.

36. Position the **mouse pointer** on the line between the two cells, and **double-click** to resize both columns to their best fit, as shown in the following illustration.

37. Position the pointer on the table's **move handle** , and then **drag** to the right to center the table under the other objects.

38. Select the **table** again, then choose the **Home→Paragraph→Border** menu button from the Ribbon.

39. Choose **No Border** from the drop-down menu to complete this page, as shown in the following illustration.

ERGONOMIC OFFICE SOLUTIONS

PRESENTS

The Ergonomically Challenged Office

What: A Luncheon Seminar
Where: The Bakery Café
When: September 27th at Noon
A catered lunch will be served

40. Save the file, and leave it **open** for the next topic.

Working with Text Boxes

Video Lesson labyrinthelab.com/videos

A text box is a special type of shape designed for you to insert text or graphics. You may wonder how inserting a text box is different from drawing a different shape and adding text inside it. It's because of the formatting. For example, when you apply a theme to a document, the theme includes formatting such as fill and line colors for shapes. Text boxes do not contain those formatting characteristics; you type in it, there is no fill color, and the text entered is left-aligned, starting at the top of the box. You can format all of the text by selecting the text box itself, or format only a portion of the text by selecting the part you want to change.

Adding a Text Box

You choose the text box from the Shapes gallery in the Illustrations group on the Insert tab and either click to place it in the document or drag it to the desired size. You can also use the Text Box gallery in the Text group on the same tab on the Ribbon to draw a text box, or choose a preformatted one from the gallery.

 If you insert the text box by clicking in the document, when you begin typing, the text box expands to the edge of the paper and then begins to wrap the text. However, if you draw the text box, it remains the same size.

Formatting a Text Box

You can format a text box just like any other object. You must first select the text box, and then you can change the line surrounding it, change the fill color, resize it, or perform any of the other options appearing on the Format tab of the Ribbon. For example, you can also apply various styles, change the direction of text, or apply shadow or 3-D effects to text boxes using the Format contextual tab. A new text box can also be saved to the Text Box Gallery.

QUICK REFERENCE	WORKING WITH TEXT BOXES
Task	**Procedure**
Insert a text box	■ Choose Text Box from the Shapes gallery.
	■ Click in the document or drag to draw to the desired size.
	or
	■ Choose Insert→Text→Text Box $\boxed{\text{A}}$ from the Ribbon.
	■ Choose a preformatted text box.
	or
	■ Choose Draw Text Box from the menu.
Format a text box	■ Select the text box.
	■ Choose the desired formatting commands from the contextual Format tab on the Ribbon.
Apply a 3-D effect	■ Select the text box.
	■ Choose Text Box Tools→Format→3-D Effects.
	■ Choose the desired effect.
Apply a shadow effect	■ Select the text box.
	■ Choose Text Box Tools→Format→Shadow Effects.
	■ Choose the desired effect.

QUICK REFERENCE	WORKING WITH TEXT BOXES (continued)
Task	**Procedure**
Apply a text box style	■ Select the text box. ■ Choose Text Box Tools→Format→Styles. ■ Choose the desired style.
Change the text direction	■ Select the text box. ■ Choose Text Box Tools→Format→Text→Text Direction. ■ Choose the desired direction.
Save a text box to the text box gallery	■ Select the text box. ■ Choose Insert→Text→Text Box. ■ Choose Save Selection to the Text Box Gallery.

DEVELOP YOUR SKILLS 9.1.2
Work with Text Boxes

In this exercise, you will insert a text box, reposition it, and format the text within it.

Insert a Text Box

1. Choose **Insert→Illustrations→Shapes** 📷 from the Ribbon.

2. Choose the **Text Box** 🅰 from the Shapes gallery.

3. Position the **Text Box mouse pointer** ╋ under the center of the WordArt object.

4. Begin dragging to draw a text box about **2 inches long** and **½ inch tall**.

5. **Type** the text shown in the illustration to the right.
   Notice how the text automatically wraps within the text box and is left-aligned.

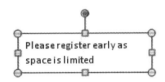

Format a Text Box

6. Follow these steps to resize the text box:

A Position the **mouse pointer** on the bottom corner of the text box. ⎯

B Drag up and right to resize the text box so it is wide enough to fit the text on one line.

7. Make sure the **text box** is selected so the contextual **Format** tab is displayed.

8. Follow these steps to remove the outline:

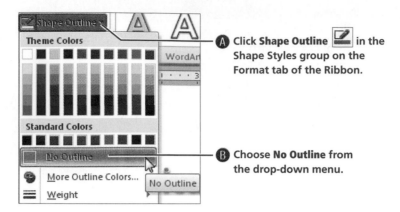

A) Click **Shape Outline** ✎ in the Shape Styles group on the Format tab of the Ribbon.

B) Choose **No Outline** from the drop-down menu.

9. Click the **Shape Fill menu button** in the Shape Styles group, and then choose **Orange, Accent 6, Lighter 80%**.

10. Choose **Drawing Tools→Format→Shape Styles→Shape Effects→3-D Rotation**.

11. Choose **Perspective Right** (the third column in the first row) in the menu.

Align Selected Objects

12. With the text box still selected, **hold down** the ⟨Shift⟩ key, and select the two objects **above** it.

13. Choose **Format→Arrange→Align** 🖫 from the Ribbon.

14. Choose **Align Center** from the menu.

15. Click in the **document** to deselect the three objects.

16. **Save** 🖫 the document, and continue with the next topic.

9.2 Working with SmartArt

Video Lesson labyrinthelab.com/videos

It is often easier to grasp concepts in business documents if information is presented graphically rather than textually. Word provides a large variety of SmartArt graphics that you can add to documents. SmartArt graphics make it easy to combine predesigned graphics with text to create sophisticated figures.

An example of a SmartArt figure

Inserting a SmartArt Graphic

When you choose Insert→Illustrations→SmartArt [icon] from the Ribbon, the Choose a SmartArt Graphic dialog box appears. This contains a large array of categorized graphic images.

Choosing a SmartArt category in the left pane displays the associated images in the center pane.

Choosing an image displays a close-up view with a description of how the image could be used.

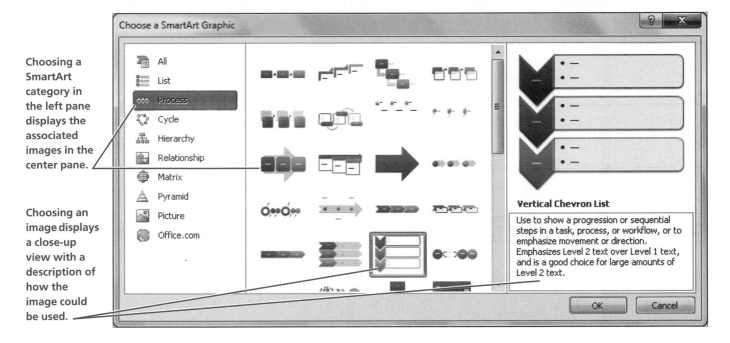

SmartArt Categories

SmartArt images are divided into the following categories:

Category	Purpose
List	Shows nonsequential data
Process	Shows steps in a process or progression
Cycle	Shows a continual process
Hierarchy	Creates a hierarchical structure or shows a decision tree
Relationship	Illustrates associations
Matrix	Shows how parts relate to a whole
Pyramid	Shows proportional relationships with the largest element on the top or bottom
Picture	Shows groups of pictures
Office.com	Shows various shapes available online

Using the SmartArt Text Pane

You use the SmartArt text pane to add text to your graphic image. When you insert the image, the text pane may or may not be open. If the pane is not open, you click the tab that appears on the left side of the image. The same tab closes the text pane. The [Text] placeholders are replaced with the text you enter in the SmartArt text pane.

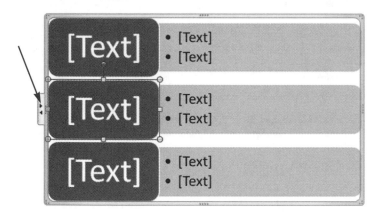

You type in a bulleted list in the Type Your Text Here pane as shown in the following illustration. As you type, the text is added to the image. Tapping Tab while entering text in the SmartArt text pane inserts the text in the right-hand column. Word adjusts the font size based on the amount of information you type. If you cannot find the exact image you want, you can modify, add, and delete Shapes within the graphic. SmartArt objects are formatted in the same way as other graphic Shapes.

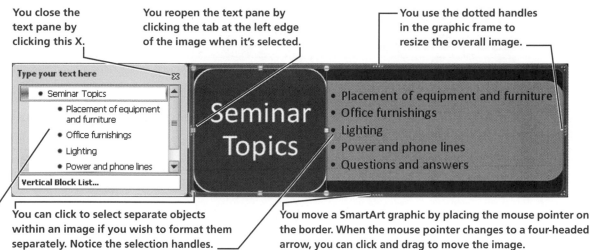

You enter the text here. You also format text in this pane, but the formatting appears only in the graphic. Sub-bullets appear in the right-hand column.

You close the text pane by clicking this X.

You reopen the text pane by clicking the tab at the left edge of the image when it's selected.

You use the dotted handles in the graphic frame to resize the overall image.

You can click to select separate objects within an image if you wish to format them separately. Notice the selection handles.

You move a SmartArt graphic by placing the mouse pointer on the border. When the mouse pointer changes to a four-headed arrow, you can click and drag to move the image.

Changing SmartArt Styles

The SmartArt Styles gallery on the contextual Design tab provides interesting variations of the original graphic. Like other galleries you have worked with, you can scroll through it, or you can use the More button to open the entire gallery. Live Preview lets you see the effect of the various styles without actually applying them.

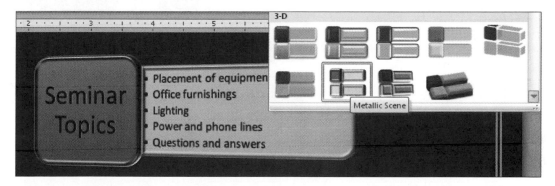

Using Live Preview to observe SmartArt Styles effects

QUICK REFERENCE	USING SMARTART
Task	**Procedure**
Insert a SmartArt image	■ Choose Insert→Illustrations→SmartArt from the Ribbon.
	■ Select the desired SmartArt category.
	■ Choose the SmartArt object you want to use, and then click OK.
Add text to a SmartArt object	■ If necessary, click the tab on the left side of the image to display the Type Your Text Here pane.
	■ Use the pane to add text to the object.
	■ To reopen the pane to add or edit text, select the object and click the tab at the left edge of the object's frame.
Apply a SmartArt Style	■ Choose Design→SmartArt Styles from the Ribbon.
	■ Click a style in the gallery to apply it to the SmartArt image.

DEVELOP YOUR SKILLS 9.2.1
Insert SmartArt

In this exercise, you will use two SmartArt graphics: one to list the seminar topics and one to list the ergonomic products.

1. **Tap** Ctrl + End to move the insertion point to the bottom of the document.

2. **Press** Ctrl + Enter to insert a page break.

3. Choose **Home→Paragraph→Center** ☰ from the Ribbon.
   Your image will be center-aligned when you insert it.

4. Choose **Insert→Illustrations→SmartArt** ⬒ from the Ribbon.

5. Follow these steps to insert a SmartArt object:

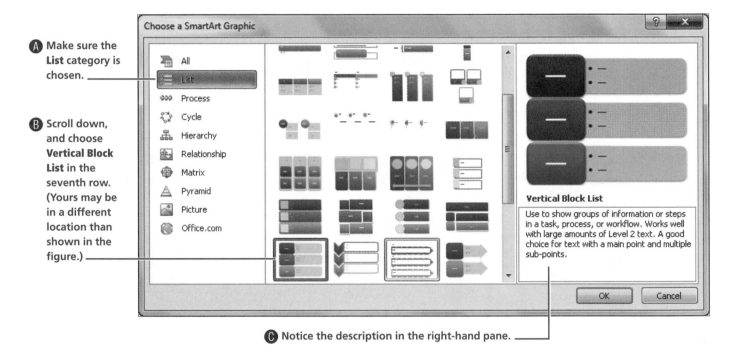

Ⓐ Make sure the **List** category is chosen.

Ⓑ Scroll down, and choose **Vertical Block List** in the seventh row. (Yours may be in a different location than shown in the figure.)

Ⓒ Notice the description in the right-hand pane.

6. Click **OK** to insert the SmartArt image in your document.

7. If the text pane is not visible, click the **tab** on the left side of the image, as shown in the following figure.

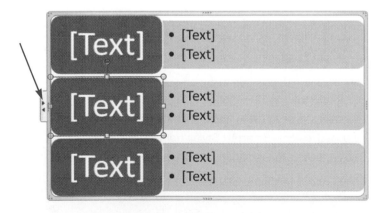

8. If necessary, reposition the **text pane** by dragging it by its top border, as shown in the following figure. In this example, it's best to position the pane to the left of the image.

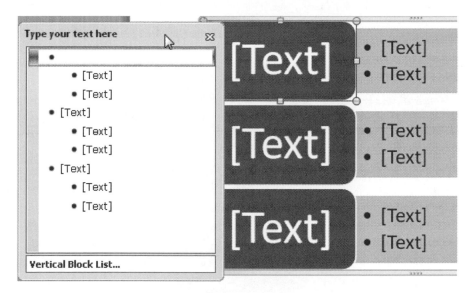

Customize the SmartArt Image

This image has three major text objects, but you will only use one.

9. If necessary, **scroll down** in the text pane until the last six bullet points are visible.

10. Follow these steps to remove two of the text objects:

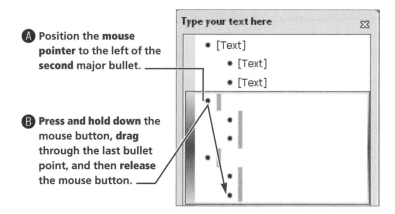

A Position the **mouse pointer** to the left of the **second** major bullet.

B Press and hold down the mouse button, **drag** through the last bullet point, and then **release** the mouse button.

11. Tap Delete to remove the last two objects.

12. Follow these steps to begin entering the seminar topics:

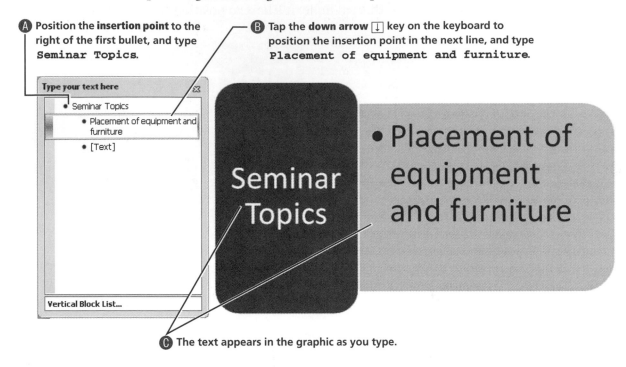

A Position the **insertion point** to the right of the first bullet, and type `Seminar Topics`.

B Tap the **down arrow** ↓ key on the keyboard to position the insertion point in the next line, and type `Placement of equipment and furniture.`

C The text appears in the graphic as you type.

13. Tap the ↓ key to go to the next line, and type **`Office furnishings`**.

14. Tap `Enter` to generate the next bulleted line, and type **`Lighting`**.

15. Tap `Enter` as necessary, and **type** the following items to complete the list:

- **`Power and phone lines`**
- **`Questions and answers`**

16. Click the **Close** ✕ button in the upper-right corner of the Type Your Text Here pane to close it.

17. Click the **outside border** of the image to make sure the entire image is selected and not just an individual object within the image.

18. Drag the **bottom-center sizing handle** up until the image is approximately half as tall as the original image.

Change the SmartArt Style

19. Choose **Design→SmartArt Styles→Change Colors** from the Ribbon.

20. In the Accent 1 category, choose the fourth column, **Gradient Loop - Accent 1**.

21. Choose **Drawing Tools→Design→ SmartArt Styles→More** button to display the entire gallery.

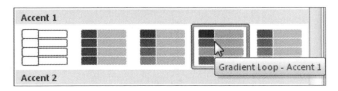

22. In the 3-D category, choose the second item in the second column, **Metallic Scene**. The Metallic Scene option may be in a different location, depending on the size of your screen.

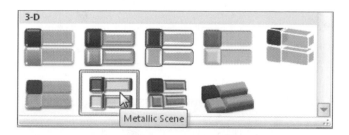

Add Another SmartArt Image

23. Tap Ctrl + End to position the insertion point at the end of the document.

24. Tap Enter twice.

25. Choose **Insert→Illustrations→SmartArt** [icon] from the Ribbon.

26. Follow these steps to insert the next image:

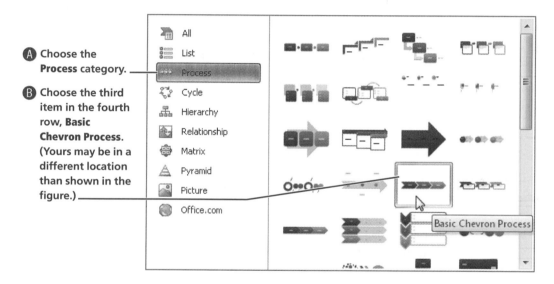

27. Click **OK** to insert the object.

28. Click on the [Text] placeholder in the first graphic arrow, and then type **Our Products**.

29. Click in each **arrow** to enter the text shown in the following illustration in the **middle** and **last arrows**.

30. If necessary, click on the **image** to select it.

31. Follow these steps to add a new arrow:

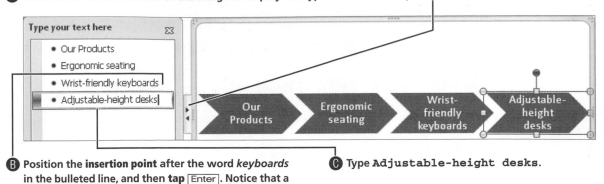

A Click the tab on the **left side** of the image to display the Type Your Text Here pane.

B Position the **insertion point** after the word *keyboards* in the bulleted line, and then **tap** Enter. Notice that a new arrow was added to the end of the graphic.

C Type **Adjustable-height desks**.

32. Close ☒ the text pane.

Format the Image

33. Click the **outside border** of the image to make sure the entire SmartArt graphic is selected.

34. Choose **Design→SmartArt Styles→Change Colors** ⬤ from the Ribbon.

35. Choose the fourth item in the Accent 1 category, **Gradient Loop – Accent 1**.

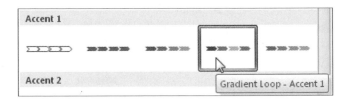

36. Click the **More** ⬇ button on the SmartArt Styles gallery, and in the 3-D category, choose the third item in the first row, **Cartoon**, and then click in the **document** to deselect the object.

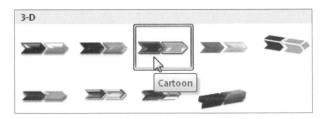

37. Save 🖫 the document, and leave it **open** for the next topic.

9.3 Formatting the Page Background

Video Lesson   labyrinthelab.com/videos

Word has great page background formatting features that add color and visual variety to your documents. Page colors and page borders provide the finishing touches that add professional polish and pizzazz. For example, you can add colors from a gallery specifically designed to blend with a document's theme. Border theme colors are also designed to tastefully complement page colors. These features are located in the Page Background group of the Page Layout tab on the Ribbon.

Adding Page Colors and Page Borders

The Page Colors gallery is similar to other color galleries you have worked with. The colors that appear in the Theme Colors section of the gallery, as the name implies, are based on the Theme currently in effect.

Page borders surround the outer edges of the entire page, rather than a particular object. You can adjust the color (again, based on the current Theme), line thickness, and other features of the border. There are also various graphic images available to use as page borders. A page border can be applied to the whole document, an individual section, the first page only, or all pages except the first page.

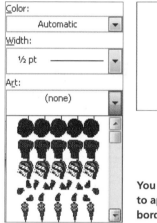 

You can choose images to appear around the border of a page.

The Borders and Shading Dialog Box

This dialog box allows you to make settings similar to those you can set for paragraphs.

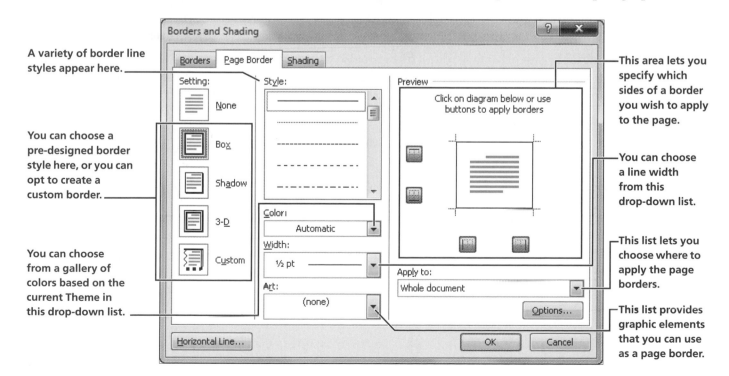

A variety of border line styles appear here.

You can choose a pre-designed border style here, or you can opt to create a custom border.

You can choose from a gallery of colors based on the current Theme in this drop-down list.

This area lets you specify which sides of a border you wish to apply to the page.

You can choose a line width from this drop-down list.

This list lets you choose where to apply the page borders.

This list provides graphic elements that you can use as a page border.

Inserting a Watermark

A watermark is text or a graphic that is placed behind the text or other objects in a document; it is visible only when in Page Layout or Full Screen Reading view and is not visible in Web, Outline, or Draft views. A watermark is inserted in the Header of a document; thus, you can apply a text watermark to the entire document or to only certain pages by inserting section breaks. Some common watermarks you may be familiar with include a faint image of the word *Draft* or *Sample* in the background or perhaps a company's logo faintly visible.

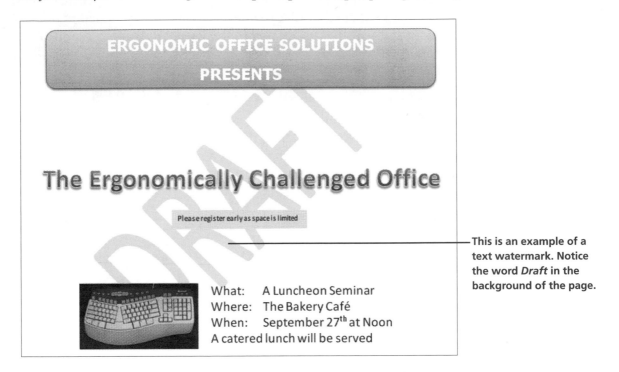

This is an example of a text watermark. Notice the word *Draft* in the background of the page.

Adding a Watermark

The watermark gallery is found in the Page Background group on the Page Layout tab of the Ribbon. There are built-in text watermarks, or you can create your own custom watermark with text or a picture. Text watermarks appear on every page, unless you specify differently. A photograph, clip art image, or picture can also be inserted by choosing Custom Watermark at the bottom of the watermark gallery, then navigating to and choosing the picture; however, the graphic will appear on every page, even if the document contains sections.

QUICK REFERENCE	FORMATTING PAGE BACKGROUNDS
Task	**Procedure**
Add a page color	■ Choose Page Layout→Page Background→Page Color from the Ribbon. ■ Choose the desired color from the gallery.

Task	Procedure
Add a page border	■ Choose Page Layout→Page Background→Page Borders ⬚ from the Ribbon. ■ Choose the desired style, color, weight, and other options from the Borders and Shading dialog box.
Add a watermark	■ Choose Page Layout→Page Background→Watermark from the Ribbon. ■ Choose the desired watermark from the gallery.
Add a picture watermark	■ Choose Page Layout→Page Background→Watermark from the Ribbon. ■ Choose Custom Watermark from the gallery. ■ Click Picture Watermark and then Select Picture. ■ Navigate to the storage location for the picture. ■ Double-click the picture to insert it.

DEVELOP YOUR SKILLS 9.3.1

Apply Page Color and a Page Border

In this exercise, you will add a background color to your brochure and a border surrounding the page. Finally, you will add a Draft watermark to the document.

Add Page Color

1. Choose **Page Layout→Page Background→Page Color** 🎨 from the Ribbon.

2. Hover the **mouse pointer** over several colors in the Theme Colors area of the gallery, and Live Preview displays the effects of the different colors.

3. Choose the color in the fifth column, bottom row, **Blue**, **Accent 1**, **Darker 50%**.

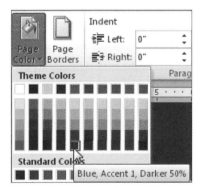

Add a Page Border

4. Choose **Page Layout→Page Background→Page Borders** ⬚ from the Ribbon.

5. Choose **Box** from the Setting area in the panel on the left.

6. Follow these steps to format the page border:

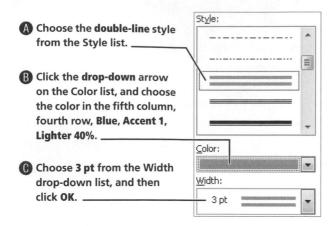

A Choose the **double-line** style from the Style list.

B Click the **drop-down** arrow on the Color list, and choose the color in the fifth column, fourth row, **Blue, Accent 1, Lighter 40%.**

C Choose **3 pt** from the Width drop-down list, and then click **OK.**

Insert a Watermark

Now, you will add a Draft watermark, and then finalize the document by removing it.

7. Choose **Page Layout→Page Background→Watermark** from the Ribbon.

8. Scroll down, and choose **Draft 1** from the watermark gallery.

9. Scroll through the document to view the watermark, page border, and page color on both pages.

10. Undo to remove the watermark from the document.

11. Save the file, and **close** it.

9.4 Concepts Review

Concepts Review labyrinthelab.com/word10

To check your knowledge of the key concepts introduced in this lesson, complete the Concepts Review quiz by going to the URL listed above. If your classroom is using Labyrinth eLab, you may complete the Concepts Review quiz from within your eLab course.

Reinforce Your Skills

Draw a Map with Shapes

In this exercise, you will use Word's Shapes to draw a map to Ergonomic Office Solutions, and you will rotate and align Shapes.

1. **Open** rs-Directions from the Lesson 09 folder.
2. Choose **View→Zoom→One Page** 📃 from the Ribbon.

Draw Lines

3. Choose **Insert→Illustrations→Shapes** 📑 from the Ribbon.
4. Choose the **first line style** in the Lines category.
5. Draw a **straight line** down the middle of the page starting about 1 inch below the rectangle and ending about 1 inch above the bottom of the page. (Remember, holding the Shift key while you draw constrains the object. This will ensure a straight line.)
6. Choose the **Line Shape** again, and draw a **horizontal line** at about the 3-inch mark on the vertical ruler, and about the same width of the rectangle.
7. Using the same method, draw **two** more **horizontal lines** of the same width at about the 5-inch and 7-inch marks on the vertical ruler.

Draw and Format a Rectangles

8. Choose **Insert→Illustrations→Shapes** 📑 from the Ribbon, and choose the **Rectangle** tool from the Rectangles category.
9. Draw a **rectangle** under the first horizontal line on the left side of the vertical line. Refer to the illustration at the end of the exercise.
10. Type **Hilliard Avenue** in the rectangle.
11. Using the same techniques, insert **two rectangles**, one below each horizontal line. *These will be used for the names of the cross streets.*
12. In the **top** rectangle, type **Brandon Road**, and in the **bottom** rectangle, type **Sycamore Avenue**.
13. Click on one rectangle, and then **hold** Shift and **click** on the other two to select all three of them.
14. Choose **Format→Shape Styles→Shape Outline** ✎ from the Ribbon, and then choose **No Outline** from the menu.
15. Choose **Page Layout→Arrange→Align** from the Ribbon, and then choose **Align Center** to align the three rectangles.

Rotate a Shape

16. Draw another **rectangle** about the same size as the others, and then type **University Avenue** in it.

17. Drag the **green rotating handle** until the rectangle is vertical.

18. Position the **mouse pointer** on an edge of the rectangle until the move handle appears, and then drag it so it is on the right side of the vertical line, similar to the illustration at the end of the exercise. Then, zoom the document back out to **100%**.

19. **Save** 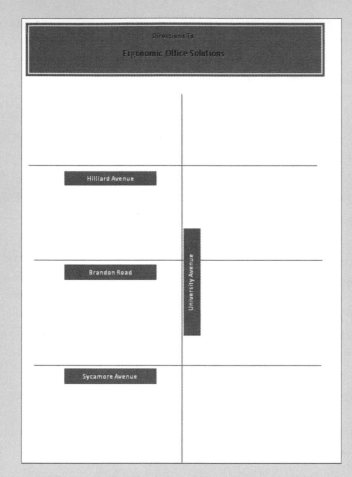 the file, and **close** it.

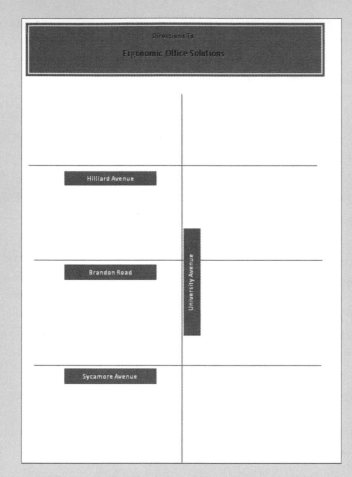

Create a Cycle Diagram Using SmartArt

In this exercise, you will create a document for your natural sciences class, picturing nature's water cycle.

1. **Open** rs-Water Cycle from the Lesson 09 folder.

2. Choose **Page Layout→Themes→Themes**  from the Ribbon.

3. Choose **Solstice** from the Themes menu.

4. Position the **insertion point** in the first line of the document.

5. Choose **Title** from the **Home→Styles→QuickStyles Gallery**.

6. **Tap** Ctrl + End to position the insertion point at the end of the document.

Insert a SmartArt Graphic

7. Choose **Insert→Illustrations→SmartArt** from the Ribbon.

8. Choose the **Cycle** category in the panel on the left side of the dialog box.

9. Choose the first diagram in the first row, **Basic Cycle**, and then click **OK** to insert the SmartArt graphic in your document.

10. If necessary, click the **tab** on the left edge of the graphic to open the Type Your Text Here pane.

11. Complete the text pane, as shown in the illustration to the right.

12. **Close** the text pane.

13. Click the **outside border** of the image to select the entire image.

Format the SmartArt Graphic

14. Choose **Design→SmartArt Styles** from the Ribbon.

15. Click the **More** button in the SmartArt Styles gallery to display the entire gallery.

16. Use **Live Preview** to examine several of the available styles, and then in the 3-D category, choose the first style in the first row, **Polished**. Finally, deselect the object.

Format the Document Background

17. Choose **Page Layout→Page Background→Page Color** from the Ribbon.

18. Choose the color in the fifth column, second row—**Aqua, Accent 1, Lighter 80%**—as the background color.

19. Choose **Page Layout→Page Background→Page Borders** from the Ribbon.

20. **Scroll down** to the black-and-white artwork, and choose the **umbrellas** from the Art drop-down list at the bottom of the center pane in the dialog box.

21. Click **OK** to place the border on the page.

22. **Save** the file, and **close** it.

Apply Your Skills

Create an Announcement

In this exercise, you will create an announcement that includes Landscape orientation, a photograph, a page border, and page color.

1. Create the announcement using the following guidelines, similar to the illustration at the end of this exercise:

   ■ Announce an upcoming concert. Include the **date**, **time**, and **location**. Also specify **where** tickets can be purchased.

   ■ List **two bands** that will be presented.

   ■ Use **Landscape** orientation.

   ■ Choose a **Theme** for your document.

   ■ **Format** the text as you desire.

   ■ **Insert** the as-Guitar Photo in the Lesson 09 folder. Format the photo as you wish.

   ■ Use a **page color** and **page border** to set off your announcement.

2. **Save** the document as **as-Announcement** in the Lesson 09 folder.

Create a Family Tree

In this exercise, you will use Shapes to create a family tree.

1. Start a **new** document, and follow these guidelines to create Helen's family tree, similar to the illustration at the end of this exercise:
   - Use a **WordArt** style of your choice to create the heading.
   - Use **rectangles**, **lines**, and **arrows** from the Shapes gallery to draw the family tree.
   - Use the **Shape Fill** colors of your choice to color the boxes.
   - Use the **Shape Outline** color of your choice to color the lines and arrows.
   - Use the illustration at the end of the exercise to add the **family names**.
   - Use **alignment tools** to align the boxes
   - Insert a **custom watermark** picture using the as-Tree Photo in the Lesson 09 folder.
   - Use your choice of **font formatting** for the family member names.
   - Apply a **page border**.

2. **Save** the file as **as-Family Tree** in the Lesson 09 folder.

Critical Thinking & Work-Readiness Skills

In the course of working through the following Microsoft Office-based Critical Thinking exercises, you will also be utilizing various work-readiness skills, some of which are listed next to each exercise. Go to labyrinthelab.com/ workreadiness to learn more about the work-readiness skills.

9.1 Create a Handout for a Report

WORK-READINESS SKILLS APPLIED

- Acquiring and evaluating information
- Seeing things in the mind's eye
- Thinking creatively

Green Clean's Purchasing Manager, Michael Chowdery, has asked you to create a handout about adding energy-efficient lighting to their product list. On the Internet, research information on the three bulbs in the ct-Light Bulbs document (Lesson 09 folder). Insert, format, and align text boxes next to each bulb listed to enter a description. If you copy information from a website, give credit for each in this manner: **Attribution: websitename.com**. Convert the title to a WordArt image of your choice and add page border. Insert and format a Shape next to the bulb you feel would be the most efficient. When finished, save and close the file.

9.2 Create an Announcement

WORK-READINESS SKILLS APPLIED

- Thinking creatively
- Seeing things in the mind's eye
- Writing

Green Clean is sponsoring a fundraiser for the WCA Garden Club, which promotes environmentally friendly gardening practices. The fundraiser will be a community yard sale held in the parking lot at Green Clean headquarters. Create an announcement for the fundraiser. Use a light page color and insert and format pictures into text boxes for a graphical impact. (Include pictures of object you might see at a yard sale.) Insert various shapes, including a SmartArt object emphasizing the details of the sale, such as where, when, and why. Highlight that this is a fundraiser. Move, resize, and align the shapes as needed. Use the ct-Garden image (Lesson 09 folder) as a watermark on the announcement. Save the file as **ct-Yard Sale**.

9.3 Create a Flyer

WORK-READINESS SKILLS APPLIED

- Organizing information
- Thinking creatively
- Seeing things in the mind's eye

Ken Hazell, the human resource manager at Green Clean, is responsible for employee training. He has arranged for a consultant to provide a half-day Word 2010 Basics class on September 22. Design a flyer to post on the bulletin board promoting the upcoming class. Include WordArt, pictures, shapes, fonts, colors, and other coordinating formats. Add a page border that coordinates with the shapes and text colors used. Use the photos in ct-School (Lesson 09 folder) or find others on the Internet. Use a SmartArt object to add three or four features you have learned in Word 2010. Save the flyer as **ct-Word Class** in the Lesson 09 folder.

Index

Notes